Boost Your Focus

Practical Strategies to Stop Postponing and Concentrate On Your Daily Goals

Jacob E. Campbell

Copyright © 2020 Jacob E. Campbell

All rights reserved.

Table of Contents

Introduction 1

Chapter 1
Focus and Concentrate – The Hidden Success Drivers 3

    What Is Concentration? 4
    Why It Is Hard to Concentrate 6
    Increasing Your Ability to Concentrate Is Possible, and These People Proved It 15
    What Concentration Can Do for You 16
    What We're Afraid of Is Failure 19

Chapter 2
Goals Matter to Focus Better 21

    Goals - What Are They and Why Do They Matter? 22
    The Four Questions You Need to Ask Yourself 26
    Goal-Setting Mistakes to Avoid 30

Chapter 3
Prioritizing Productive Habits and Schedules 37

    What Are Habits? 37
    The Current Habits That Are Killing Your Productivity .. 38
    How to Break Out of Old Habits 44
    Building Better Habits for Greater Productivity 46

Chapter 4
Turbocharge Your Focus with the Targeted Approach to Overcoming Procrastination 53

    Understanding Your Procrastination Tendencies 53
    How to Stop Procrastinating and Switch On Your Focus 62
    Rely on the Pomodoro Technique 67

Chapter 5
Getting Rid of Other Common Distraction Factors 71

The Science Behind Distraction 71
How Distraction Has Become A Problem 75
The Underestimated Distraction You Didn't Think Of..... 79
More Tried and True Techniques to Boost Your Ability to
Concentrate.. 84

Chapter 6
Creating A Working System Just for You 91

Optimizing Your Mind and Body for Better Your Ability to
Concentrate and Focus 92
How to Train Your Brain for Laser-Sharp Focus.............. 97
How to Sharpen That Attention Span 102

Conclusion 109

Introduction

Congratulations on purchasing *Boost Your Focus,* and thank you for doing so.

What is the secret to success? That is the question that plagues so many of us. We *know* that we want to succeed. If given a choice, we would like to embody all the traits that successful people have too. They got to where they are by doing something right, and the question is, *what did they do that made a difference?* The answer lies in their ability to focus and concentrate.

To achieve a goal that is set, you must have an incredible ability to focus. You must develop the ability to tune out and block out the external noise and distraction and harness the ability to focus no matter what circumstances you find yourself in. The ones who were able to hold on to their level of concentration were the ones who went on to succeed. When director James Cameron was asked what led to his ability to create incredible movies like *Titanic* and *Avatar,* he replied that focus had a lot to do with it. Cameron said to get anything worthwhile done, you must be able to focus like a laser. That same sentiment is shared by many successful people. But what does it mean to *focus and concentrate?*

Success requires a single-minded focus. Focus and the ability to concentrate gives you the ability to achieve any specific goal that you may have set for yourself. More importantly, it gives you the ability to focus on this goal long enough to see it through all the way to the end. Larry Page, the co-founder of Google, once said that you need to be single-minded about any important goal that you set for yourself if you want to achieve it. This statement highlights the very reason that so many people fail to achieve the goals that they set for themselves. It is not because they were not capable, but because they did not have the ability to stay focused long enough to finish what they set out to do. It is very easy to let yourself get carried away by the distractions that surround your life day in and day out. Therefore, you need concrete and effective strategies on your side to help you boost your powers of concentration. Andrew Carnegie summed it up nicely when he said, *"Concentration and focus means that you are putting all your eggs into one basket and then watching that basket.* If you're ready to get rid of the distractions and find that ability to focus with determination and commitment to every task that you take on, then this book is meant for you.

There are plenty of books on this subject on the market, thanks again for choosing this one! Every effort was made to ensure it is full of as much useful information as possible, please enjoy!

Chapter 1

Focus and Concentrate – The Hidden Success Drivers

"All the world's a stage, and the men and women in it are merely players. They have their exits and their entrances, and one person in their lifetime can play many parts" - William Shakespeare; As You Like It.

What an incredibly powerful statement, and so profound in the way that it relates to our capacity to concentrate. Shakespeare's powerful metaphor can serve as a framework for understanding our ability to concentrate. You are an actor, and the world that you live in is your stage. The perfect show that you display on stage is the result of highly focused attention. Like many plays, a great show happens when all the actors know their parts and come together to create a seamless performance. An actor knows their role, the part they need to play, and performs that role accordingly. An actor who does not know their role or their lines is doomed to have a poor performance. In your world, every task that you take on is your purpose, and knowing what you need to do is how you execute each task perfectly. What you are struggling with now is staying focused on your purpose long enough without getting distracted or sidetracked along the way.

Like an actor who plays many parts, you will have many tasks that you need to handle each day. While the tasks themselves may not be difficult, the ability to concentrate is. Some people find it difficult to even concentrate for five minutes without getting distracted. Try this quick exercise. Pick up a book and try to focus on reading that book alone for ten minutes. Do nothing else except read the next few pages in front of you for the next ten minutes. How did you go? Were you able to concentrate? Or did you find yourself thinking about several things while you were doing that task? Living in the twenty-first century with an abundance of distractions has led us to believe that we need to be super productive to live a fulfilling life. Yet, for some reason or another, most people find that their productivity levels are extremely low.

Not being able to focus can be extremely frustrating. When you have a lot to get done, and you know that you're running out of time, yet you still struggle to find the willpower to concentrate long enough, it can start to get to you. The inability to concentrate is a multilayered problem, and like all problems, there is always an underlying cause. You know that you want to start focusing better on the things that matter most. The question is, what can you do about it?

What Is Concentration?
Depending on the context, your ability to concentrate can have several meanings. In the context of being able to complete tasks with minimal distraction, your ability to concentrate refers to the ability to maintain clarity of the mind. It is the mind's ability to remain free and clear of anything else except the task that is in front of you. It is about the ability to channel all your thoughts and energy into that one, single task, and to think about nothing else until that task

is completed. Although it would appear that way, your ability to concentrate is not a state of mind. Not initially, at least. It is about deliberate action because you need to deliberately focus all your attention on a single task, and then maintain that focus while blocking out everything else around you.

Concentration is a term that is sometimes used interchangeably with other words like attention and focus, but they always lead back to the same result. Your ability to focus is something that needs to be strengthened and developed with time. There is no magic formula or one-size-fits-all solution, and there is a simple reason for this. Every individual is unique, and this means that everyone has their own style of working. Some techniques work better than others for certain individuals, and the aim of this book is to help you discover the techniques that work best for you. Your ability to develop your concentration is going to depend on your ability to adapt and willingness to change your mindset too. It is an ability that can be improved on, but it is going to take time, and change is not going to happen overnight.

Concentration is not a special talent. It is not a gift or special ability that only some people are blessed enough to be born with. Concentration is about your thoughts and the way that you think them. We all have the capacity, the energy, and the inner drive that is needed to be successful in anything that we undertake. The trouble that most people struggle with is not knowing *how to tap into* these inner capabilities. There is a very valid reason that many of the most successful people in the world attribute their success to the ability to concentrate because it is an important skill that everyone should possess. It is meant to help you stay on track to achieving your goals and reaching your full potential. Without that extra push, that necessary kick in the butt, many of us would be guilty of slacking off far too much and taking things easy. Concentration is a necessary skill that will help relieve your mind of distracting thoughts long enough for you to achieve your goals.

Why It Is Hard to Concentrate

You're not the only one who struggles to find the focus that you need to complete a project or task that you're supposed to be working on. Many people struggle through this very same challenge. The difference is, not everyone knows what they can do to fix the problem or where they can even begin working on overcoming this challenge. It can be immensely frustrating when you look around at other people and see how focused they can be on their tasks. When you're working in an office setting, and you see your coworkers' are busy typing away furiously at their keyboards while you struggle to form a single sentence, it can be nerve-wracking. You can't help but wonder what it is you're doing wrong and why you find it so hard to stay focused. The problem is not you. Well, not entirely anyway. The problem is you don't fully *understand why* you're so easily distracted and find it hard to maintain your ability to concentrate. *That is the first problem.* When we don't understand what we are up against, we will not be able to find the solutions that we need to fix it. Trying to fix a problem that you don't understand is going to be like stumbling around in the dark without a torchlight in hand. How do you know where you're going or what is going to work when you don't know what you're doing because you can't see it?

The human mind struggles with the ability to concentrate. One of the biggest challenges that we find difficult to overcome is Instant gratification, one of life's biggest enemies, and it is the reason that we fall off the wagon on the course to achieving success. The thought of having access to immediate pleasure now, instead of sacrificing and waiting for that pleasure to present itself in the future, is a thought that not many are able to resist. This becomes a form of distraction, and distraction will always have only one outcome. The inability to concentrate. There is also the fact that our mind is full of disturbing thoughts. These are the thoughts that threaten to tear us away from what we should be concentrating on. Distracting thoughts like feeling worried that you're never going to be good enough no matter how hard you try will prevent you from trying at all, and before you know it, you're procrastinating or making excuses about why you can't get started. Disturbing thoughts threaten to pull away from your ability to concentrate by focusing on the distant future. Instead of thinking about what you should be doing now, your mind is too busy thinking about what you want to achieve. While it is not wrong to think about your future, it does present a problem when your mind is focused too much on it to the point that you can't stay focused long enough in the present to finish the job.

In a world filled with new waves and trends, the ability to concentrate is becoming more overlooked by the day. Despite its great value, it is not given enough credit because we're too distracted by all the other stimuli. We don't think about how beneficial your ability to concentrate can be, and we're certainly not thinking about the reasons behind the lack of concentration we experience. Recognizing the latter, however, is the first step to overcoming the conundrum. The difficulty in staying focused can be attributed to several reasons:

- **You're Not Getting Enough Sleep** - Your body and mind need to recharge, and when it's not getting the rest that it needs, you're going to find it a lot more difficult to get through your day. The simplest of tasks will seem to require a lot of effort. If getting through the day is a struggle, imagine how much harder it is going to be to harness the laser-sharp focus that you need when your mind and body are not cooperating? Not getting enough sleep can put a serious damper on your ability to focus. Not even ten cups of coffee throughout the day is going to make a difference when you're not fixing what is wrong from the *inside*. When you're sleep-deprived, your focus is limited because your brain is confused and tired. By not getting enough sleep the night before, you're not giving your brain enough time to prepare itself for the day ahead, let alone the challenges that it needs to face. You've had those days when you didn't get enough sleep the night before, and the next day, all you could think about was shutting down and how badly you wanted the day to be over so you could crawl into bed and shut your eyes. If you think that you're getting more than the adequate amount of sleep you need and yet, still find yourself tired the next day, you might want to consider consulting your doctor. You could be struggling with a sleep deprivation condition, and it is worth getting this checked out if it is affecting your ability to focus. Getting enough sleep at night is not about clocking in the right amount of hours alone. What you need is deep, restful, REM sleep. Eight hours of sleep at night is not going to help if that sleep is interrupted and you're restless throughout the night.

- **You're Not Getting Enough Exercise** - A lack of rest is not the only problem that is affecting your ability to concentrate. Not getting enough movement or exercise throughout a day is also a problem. Regular exercise keeps your body healthy and stimulates both the mind and the body. When your mind and body are in peak health, your ability to concentrate is automatically improved. Exercise is something that is all too easily forgotten about and cast aside these days in favor of a busy work schedule. It is easy to say that you don't have time to fit in thirty minutes of exercise when you've already got a full plate to juggle. But the consequences of *not getting enough exercise* are going to take its toll on both your mind and your body. Did you know that regular exercise is the key to promoting your brain's plasticity? Exercising boosts your hormones and minimizes the stress that you feel. It helps to increase your sensitivity to insulin while helping to keep anxiety and depression at bay. There are so many benefits to getting enough regular exercise that it is worth carving out some time in your schedule to commit to this. All of the benefits can affect your ability to concentrate, and if you want your mind and body to work a lot more efficiently, it is time to find ways to get moving.

- **You're Surrounded by Too Many Distractions -** We are all too familiar with this one since we live in a world that is filled with distractions from the moment we wake up in the morning. Our lives have become wonderfully advanced, and while that has brought a lot of benefits, it has also become the main cause of our distraction. Most people today are very likely to interact on more than one device at a time. This means that you could be on your laptop while responding to a text or email at the same time. You've probably done this a few times yourself, where you're typing away at something only to have your phone beep with a notification. You pause, pick up your phone, respond, and perhaps scroll through social media while you're half paying attention to the task you were working on your laptop before. Another common example of how distracted we have become today is having the TV running while you're using your phone or computer. This is another habit that you will find has become all too common these days. When was the last time you watched a movie all the way through without picking up your phone once or twice? We have become so accustomed to this lifestyle that we don't realize how it is splitting our focus. It contributes to the inability to concentrate, and the problem is most people don't see this as a problem at all. We have convinced ourselves that we are able to multitask, but the truth is we're struggling to stay focused today more than ever. This distraction is even spilling over into our real-life relationships too. When we're talking to someone, we *think* we are giving them our undivided attention, but if you have your phone in your hand, half scrolling and talking, you're not really paying attention at all. There are too many sources of stimulation, and that has presented a major challenge where maintaining prolonged concentration is concerned. What you need to do is stop and consider the very real possibility that your devices are hindering your ability to focus, despite how much you try to convince yourself that you can handle it.

- **Your Work Environment Is Too Messy** - Someone who can work quickly and efficiently in a messy workspace is someone who is definitely in the minority group. Most people cannot do this because a messy environment is a distraction. It is true that some creative types of personalities are at their most productive when they are surrounded by a messy workstation, but if this is not you, then this is one of the reasons why you find it so difficult to stay focused on a single task. Perhaps it is time you took a good look around at your current workspace. Does it need some order and organization? A messy workspace might not bother you on a conscious level, but it is definitely bothering you on a subconscious level. You need to clear out your workstation and free it from the papers, folders, cluttered knickknacks, and random pieces of items that are all over this space. All of it is nothing more than a distraction for your brain. Of course, nobody has an absolutely spotless workspace, and you are more than welcomed to personalize your workspace in the way that works best for you. What you do need to do, however, is to make sure you have enough free space to easily focus on a task while you're working.

- **You Don't Have A Plan** - You need to have a plan for the tasks that you're going to tackle. Going with the flow or trying to wing it and see what happens is never an approach that is going to be effective. Sure, once in a while, it might work, and you might get lucky, but lucky streaks are something that never lasts for long. For every task that you need to take on, especially the important ones that require your ability to concentrate, you need to have a plan of action that will serve as your guiding framework. When you know the steps you need to take, it makes you a lot more efficient. Mechanics have a plan of action before they start working on a car. Doctors have a plan of action and a process that they work through when you come in for a visit. No task is ever too small to have a concrete plan. A plan can be something as small as a checklist for your trip to the grocery store or something more comprehensive, like drawing out the step by step process for your next big assignment. Regardless of how or what you choose to do to prepare for the tasks you need to do, preparation is the key to making it happen. Sometimes, the brain can feel overwhelmed when a task seems too big, and this makes it difficult to stay focused. Breaking the steps down into smaller action steps makes it much easier to process. The easier your brain believes something is, the easier it will eventually become as your ability to concentrate increases.

- **You're Not Dealing with Problems** - Are you the kind of person who avoids confronting their problems because it is too unpleasant to deal with? Or perhaps you're hoping the problem will go away on its own if you ignore it long enough. Problems are something we all have to deal with, and yes, they can be unpleasant. But ignoring your problems is not going to fix anything, and it is certainly not helping your ability to stay focused. When you ignore the problem, you will notice that your mind still continues to think about the problem and how you need to address it. Yet, you never do anything about it because you can't bring yourself too. As long as the problem persists, it's going to weigh on your mind, even when you try to distract yourself by doing other tasks. The problem is going to become your distraction. Until it is fixed and a solution has been found, your mind is always going to wander back to the problem, and you won't be able to concentrate until you do something about it. You need to do something about it, even if the problem can't be fixed right away. Putting it down on your to-do list as a task to be tackled later is one example of something that you can do right away. The simple act of writing it down can do a lot to help clear your mind and re-center your focus.

- **You're Working Too Hard** - All work and no play is not good for your health or your brain. A lot of people today spend more time working than they should, and their ability to concentrate is now paying the price for it. In the old days before the Internet, computers, laptops, and mobile technology, we would go to work, clock in, and at the end of the day, clock out and get some much-needed rest. We could do this because there was no way for us to bring our work home with us. Today, work doesn't stop even after you have left the office, and this is a reality for a lot of people. With everything accessible on our mobile phones, it is now even harder than ever to separate our work lives from our personal lives. Emails and work notifications keep coming in well into the night and even on your days off. You need to step away from work every now and again because this is going to be beneficial to your mental and physical health. Don't ignore your body when you're struggling to concentrate, it is trying to tell you that it is time for a break. Listen to your body and take your inability to concentrate anymore as a sign that it is time to shut off for a little while until you're fresh again. If you try to do too much and push yourself to work at every available hour you can, it is only going to cause your ability to focus to deteriorate. Your brain is tired, and unlike your computer, it cannot go on for hours without some rest in between. You will ultimately become a lot less efficient at anything that you do when you're pushing yourself too hard all the time. If you want to improve your ability to concentrate, and it is time to get serious about taking breaks in between.

- **Your Diet Is Unhealthy** - For your boy and your mind to function properly, it needs the right fuel to keep it going. Think of your body as a car, without the right gas, it is not going to start or move anywhere. Not for long, at least. Like every machine out there, your body is a working machine too and giving your body the wrong type of fuel is going to lead to problems. An occasional treat every now and then is fine, but if you want your body and mind to function at optimal capacity, you need to start getting serious about your diet. Drinking more water, eating more fruits and vegetables, and fueling your body with vitamins is going to be beneficial in the long run. There is no need to go on extreme diets or become a health nut, all you need to do is make better choices about your nutrition.

- **You're Under Too Much Stress** - With the fast-paced and demanding world that we live in today, suffering from too much stress can be applied to pretty much everyone. We all have some sort of anxiety, worry, or angst that troubles us. Some people struggle with more than their fair share of worries every single day, and it is deeply affecting their ability to stay focused and concentrate. There is no need to point out how terrible stress can be for both your mind and your body. While you may not be able to eliminate the cause of that stress entirely (depending on what you're dealing with), finding ways to cope is the next best approach that is going to help you immensely. Meditation, yoga, deep breathing exercises, taking naps, going for a walk, there are a lot of little ways to help minimize the stress in your life. What you are trying to do is to keep the stress manageable and stop it from taking over your mind too much until it affects your ability to concentrate. With less stress and worries in your life, your ability to concentrate is easier to come by.

- **You Could Have ADHD -** Undiagnosed ADHD could be a hidden problem that you might be struggling with if you have tried every technique you can think of and still find it hard to concentrate. If you have trouble listening to other people when they're talking to you, difficulty prioritizing your tasks, or following instructions, then it could be that you're struggling with ADHD that you didn't know about. If you're irritable and often restless, it could be an underlying symptom of ADHD too. If this applies to you, then you are going to have a lot more trouble focusing than other people would. If you think this might be a problem that you're dealing with, it is best to talk to your doctor about it and get a proper diagnosis. There are ways to treat the condition with professional help.

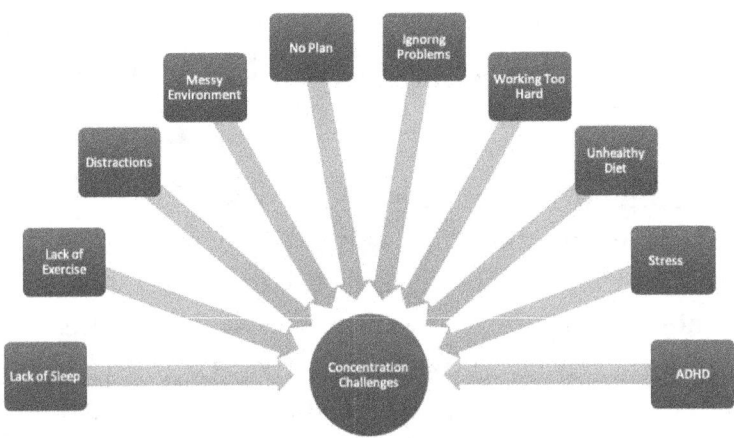

Increasing Your Ability to Concentrate Is Possible, and These People Proved It

The ability to concentrate may seem like an impossible skill to master, but if there is anything that history has taught us, it is that nothing is impossible. Anything is possible if you want it badly enough, including your ability to stay focused. Successful people throughout history have proved what amazing accomplishments can be achieved when you have a single-minded focus to guide your way. Albert Einstein, for example, didn't let his challenges and setbacks stop him. He used his ability to focus as a method to become one of the most intellectual and fascinating figures in history while making unique contributions to the world of physics. Beethoven became deaf at the age of twenty, but he did not let them stop him from concentrating on his true passion. He focused on his music and nothing else, and he could do this so well that he could hear his symphonies in his mind. Bill Gates, Warren Buffet, Elon Musk, Steve Jobs, Mark Zuckerberg, Oprah, all of these famous names share more than just success stories that have served as an inspiration for many. They share the ability to concentrate so well on what needs to be done that they don't let anything else distract them until they have achieved their purpose in life. The one thing that the rest of us share in common is that we want to know how they did it.

What Concentration Can Do for You

With pure focus and the ability to concentrate, you can become unstoppable. You are able to get more done in a day than most people get done in a week if you wanted to. All because you learned how to stay focused on a task for a prolonged period without getting distracted the way that you did before. Learning how to concentrate and concentrate well every day is a *must*. Why? Because when you lose yourself in a task and become so immersed in your work, you become a lot more productive. That has a ripple effect, and the more productive you become, the less stressed you feel when you see your workload diminishing steadily. Your happiness then increases because you're getting more done, and your performance improves when your productivity and motivation levels increase. You become a better student or employee when this happens, and this will encourage you to keep the momentum going.

The ability to focus and concentrate can yield great benefits for your overall quality of life. This, at the end of the day, is how many successful people got to where they are. They are enjoying the quality of life that most people dream about by finding balance and the ability to harness their powers and your ability to concentrate when they needed to. They discovered the benefits of what their ability to concentrate meant and what it could do for them. This is how your ability to concentrate can help you achieve greater success and control over your life:

- When you concentrate, you can take control of the things that you do. When you are not concentrating, your tasks and the distractions around you end up *controlling you.*

- When you concentrate on something and channel all your energy on that task, you handle that task in a much better, more organized manner.

- Inner focus and your ability to concentrate will give you the ability to mentally block out the distractions through awareness.

- The ability to concentrate will help you harness positive energy in your body, allowing you to gain control when you experience a negative spiral by putting things into perspective. This will dramatically reduce those moments when you find yourself feeling overwhelmed.

- Your ability to concentrate will help you develop the ability to focus on the positive to change your perspective. With the enhanced ability to concentrate, you will become better at choosing what you want to pay attention to. Since focusing on the negative is what we have a predisposition to, negativity will only make everything seem worse than it is. With the ability to concentrate, you will be able to detach yourself from the negative and reinvest in that focus into something beneficial.

- Your ability to concentrate will refine your problem-solving abilities. When you can't concentrate, you will always find it difficult to power through a problem. People focus on problems differently. One person may focus on the reasons behind the problems, while another might focus on the solutions to the problems instead. Through your ability to concentrate, you will learn how to focus on the solutions instead, and this will yield significantly better results.

- Through your ability to concentrate, your decision-making skills will become enhanced. Most people don't realize that our ability to make decisions is a crucial success factor in life, and the right choices cannot be made without the ability to concentrate on the right factors. The right decisions cannot be made until you are entirely focused on the problem and its solutions, and more importantly, you're concentrating on all the right information to help you make the right decision.

- Your ability to concentrate will harness and strengthens your determination and willpower. When you witness for yourself what removing distractions can do for your productivity, your determination and willpower are going to increase as a result. Distractions are the pitfall on your way to success. Yes, even the most common distractions like social media, for example, can make the completion of any task impossible.

- When you concentrate, there is a better chance that you are going to finish what you started. You will no longer entertain the idea of procrastination anymore because you will be concentrating on getting things done instead. The sooner you get it done, the sooner you get to cross it off your to-do list and move on to other things.

- Your ability to concentrate and the ability to get things done will generate a greater sense of satisfaction. When you see the items on your to-do list getting crossed off and completed one by one as you smash through each task, you're going to feel satisfied and proud of yourself.

- Your ability to concentrate keeps you focused on the finish line ahead. Eyes on the prize, as the old saying goes. When you're able to do this, your brain and your heart will finally be in sync, giving you the superpower that you need to plow through and not quit until it's done.

- Your ability to concentrate helps you build momentum. With your productivity and efficiency on the rise, you progress much faster through your tasks. The quicker you get your stuff done in a day, the more time you will have to relax, unwind, and spend time on the things and people you care about.

What We're Afraid of Is Failure

We don't procrastinate or find it difficult to concentrate because we're afraid of the hard work that is involved. No, the truth is, most people are afraid of the possibility of failure. The fear of failure triggers procrastination, and that procrastination contributes to your inability to concentrate on what you know you should be doing. The only way you can fail at something is if you don't try at all. You're not a failure if you need to work on improving something. That's what every successful person has had to do on their way to the top.

When your goals are not articulated, it becomes difficult to concentrate on the ways you need to achieve them. Therefore, your ability to concentrate is the only way to enhance your engagement in anything that you undertake. You may not like what you have to do at times, but when you're concentrating on something bigger, like the end goal you have in mind, you will be able to dig deep and find the focus capabilities you need.

BOOST YOUR FOCUS

Chapter 2

Goals Matter to Focus Better

Steve Jobs made a very inspirational speech in 2005 at the Stanford Commencement. In his speech, he made some very pivotal points about life, and it went a little something like this: *"Since then, for the past thirty-three years, I have looked in the mirror every morning and asked myself, if today were the last day of my life, would I want to do what I am about to do today? By remembering that I will be dead soon, it is one of the biggest tools I have used to help me make the important choices in life"*. These are powerful words from what was arguably a legendary man. In his speech, he was talking about his ability to focus and what he drew on to help him achieve the focus and the ability to concentrate he needed to succeed. Apple would not be the company that it was today if it wasn't for his driven determination. Jobs knew how to strip away everything else and only concentrate on what was essential, and this desire to minimize distractions even translated into his everyday life where he lived as a minimalist. This concept even translated into his products, and the Apple range is the legacy that is left behind. Functional products that strip away everything else but the essential.

The ability to concentrate is the driving force behind many successful entrepreneurs today. If you sat down with all of them and asked how they achieved the things that they did, the ability to concentrate is going to be among the answers that you get back. The ability to concentrate, along with having goals, are the two factors that will bring about the biggest transformation in this early stage as you try to build the focus skills you need. If you have set goals in the past that you didn't quite achieve, then you might think of goals as a very frustrating process. The idea of having goals might even make you feel demotivated if you have set them in the past but didn't achieve any of the goals you set out to do. You might be thinking, *"What is the point of setting goals when you're not going to achieve them?"*. But that is where you would be wrong.

Goals - What Are They and Why Do They Matter?

Goals will give you clarity in your life. With this clear image in your mind, you will know the path that you need to take and what you need to do to get there. This goal is giving you a sense of purpose, a direction to head toward. When you have this clear path to take, it makes it easy to concentrate on the next step forward instead of being distracted by all the things that could go wrong. When you concentrate on nothing but the next step, blocking out the thoughts that make you doubt yourself will become a lot easier after a while. The human mind needs something else to latch on to before it can shift away from the other distracting thoughts, and a goal gives it something else to latch on to.

It is important to point out that there is a very big difference between dreams and goals. For example, you can dream about being rich and famous, but it doesn't necessarily mean you will become rich and famous. Not unless you do something about it, and that "something" is having goals. You need to formulate a plan of action to get you from where you are now to the dream that you want to turn into reality. A goal is your blueprint for taking your dream and making it a reality. That is the true purpose of a goal. It is not there to remind you of the things that feel impossible to achieve. It is not there to be demotivated. Quite the opposite, in fact, because when harnessed correctly, your goal is going to be the very thing that changes the course of your life when it is combined with your ability to concentrate skills needed to help you stay on track. The only way to gain clarity about your goals is to write them down and break them down into steps. One goal should have one, two, three, or more steps involved before you can consider that goal done and dusted.

If you need even more reasons to convince you why goals matter, take a look at some of these:

- **Goals Keep You Motivated -** How many resolutions have you made for yourself at the start of every year? Goals like *I want to start going to the gym more, I want to lose ten kilos, I want to start eating healthier.* How many of those resolutions did you accomplish by the end of that year? The time that you set those resolutions or goals for yourself does not matter. You could set them at the start of every year, halfway through the year, at the end of the year, it does not matter. What matters here is finding the motivation to do what you initially set out to do. Setting goals was not the problem. The problem was that you lacked the motivation and the ability to concentrate you needed to start. A goal helps to keep the end objective in mind, and when you can see the finish line, you give your mind something to concentrate on. What you should do when you struggle is to use your goals as a reminder of why you are doing this. Use them as a reminder as to why you got started. Use them as a reminder of why you need to push through these hard, challenging parts when every part of your brain is telling you to give up and quit.

- **Goals Carve Out Your Path** - A goal helps to carve out the path that you need to take. The only thing that is left is for you to place your attention on that path and concentrate on what needs to come next. In a world that is full of distraction and noise, it can be hard to keep your attention on what it is that you truly desire. Well, that is what your goals are for. Your resources are limited. Your time, money, and energy are not an endless supply. If you want to truly change the course of your life, you need to channel your resources toward the avenues that matter. This means that you cannot afford to get distracted when you know that you have a goal to achieve. The fastest and surest way to get what you want in life is to take advantage of the resources that you have and forget about the distractions, at least for the time being. You don't have to neglect social media to stay away from your mobile phones, emails, and text messages forever, but while you're tapping into your resources, it is best to put these distractions aside for the time being. When you struggle to do it, turn to your goals once again as a reminder.

- **Goals Help to Make You Accountable** - When you feel like you are obligated to carry out what you promised to someone, you're more likely to stick to that commitment and see it through. Think of your goals as a commitment that you make to yourself. Right now, you have an obligation to yourself to commit to what you promised, but having goals alone is not going to be enough to motivate you to stick to them. Oh no, what you need to do is *tell other people* about the goals that you want to achieve. *This* will make you accountable. When you tell other people about your goals, like a friend, family member, spouse, or partner, it makes you feel like you are now obligated to do what you said you were going to do. By speaking your goals out loud, you put yourself in a position where you have to answer to others when they ask you how you're progressing along. Without a goal, there's no sense of urgency to achieve what you need to within a certain timeframe. It can be an eye-opening experience when you look back at the goals you set for yourself in the past but didn't quite accomplish. It can make you feel guilty too, when you look back and you wish that you had done more if only you had been more accountable. When you realize that you could have done it if only you had been more committed, the new goals you set for yourself will strengthen your resolve as you take on that responsibility knowing that success is entirely in your hands right now. This feeling of being accountable for your goals is going to make you think twice about abandoning your plans. In fact, knowing that you have to answer for your progress is going to give you that added boost of focus you need. When you stay accountable for your goals, you stay accountable for your dreams and desires.

- **Goals Push You to Become the Best Version of Yourself -** Each time that you achieve a goal, you are proving to yourself that you had it in you all along. You had it in you to be the successful person you have always dreamed of becoming. The goals that we set will always be goals that make us better than the person we are today. No one is going to set a goal for themselves that will make them a worse version of themselves. Goals move us forward, not backward, and that is why they push us to become the best version of ourselves that we can be. When you know what you want to achieve and why you need to do it, it makes you mentally more resilient against the challenges that come your way. Without a goal and a purpose, it would be all too easy to give in to the temptation of giving up. Goals give you the level of productivity and the motivation that you need to keep moving forward. Each time you see yourself inching closer to a goal you thought was impossible in the beginning, your confidence is increased bit by bit. With each challenge or obstacle you overcome, your belief in your ability to do this is renewed. There are very few people in this world who manage to accomplish everything that they set out to do. Knowing that you're one of those people who are close to achieving success can be an extremely empowering feeling. Once you have had a taste of this feeling, you will keep wanting more. The desire to repeat the emotional high from that sense of accomplishment will be just what you need to help you concentrate on achieving every goal you set for yourself.

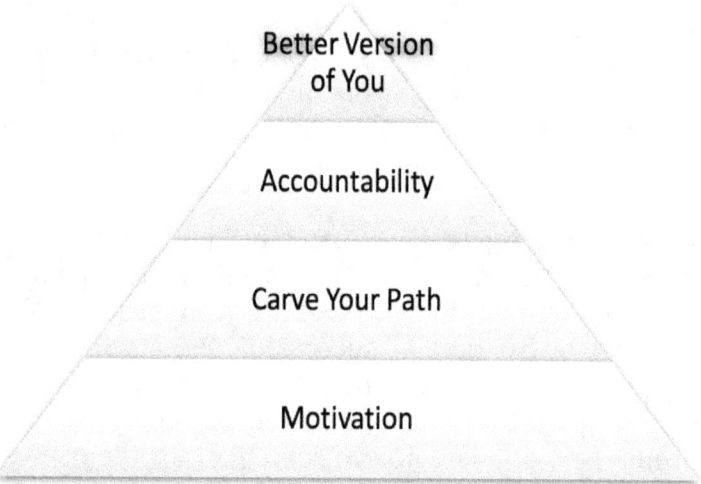

The Four Questions You Need to Ask Yourself

In 1979, students of the Harvard MBA program were asked by interviewers how many of them actually set goals. It turns out that eighty-four percent of those enrolled in the program set no goals at all, while thirteen percent of them set goals, but they were not committed to putting those goals down on paper. Only three percent of those enrolled in the MBA program set goals that they wrote down on paper, along with the plans to accomplish those goals. Ten years later, the same individuals were interviewed again in 1989, and the results were amazing. It turns out that the thirteen percent who had goals but didn't write them down on paper was still doing twice as well as the eighty-four percent of them who did not have any goals at all. What was even more incredible was the fact that the three percent of those individuals who had committed to writing those goals down on paper was making *more money* than the two other groups combined. This makes it very clear that goals *do make a difference, after all.*

When you're setting goals for yourself, there are three questions you need to ask:

- **Are Your Goals Too Vague?** - Are your goals specific enough? Becoming more specific about the goals that you want to achieve means that you are more likely to understand how much planning is going to be involved in terms of time and resources. It will also give you enough time to plan your resources wisely and figure out how you can fit your goals around the rest of your schedule in a day or a week. Always try to make your goals as specific as possible. The more details you can include in your goals, the better.

- **Are Your Goals Far Too Grand to Be Achievable?** - This one is a very valid question. While you should dream big and reach for the stars, your goals still need to be realistic *to your current situation.* Bill Gates summed it up best when he said, *"People often overestimate what they can do in one year, and underestimate what they can do in ten years."* It can be tempting to try and push for a bigger change quickly by trying to do it all at once. Instead, what you should be doing is working in stages. You need to form the building blocks that will eventually lead to the much grander goal, but for the immediate future, your goals should be realistic to the current time, resources, and situation that you find yourself in. Instead of going for grand straight away, try to find digestible work blocks instead. Think of every block that you build right now as leading to something bigger and better in the future. The little actions that you take right now are all going to culminate into the change that you want in the future, but instead of overwhelming your brain right away, you're breaking it down into smaller, actionable steps that *can be achieved*. Your brain needs to believe that it can achieve the goal you set, or it is going to have a hard time getting started.

- **Are You Currently Surrounded by the Right Kind of People?** - Are you being influenced by the right kind of people? The company that you keep matters more than you think. This is because the people that you surround yourself with are going to have an impact on whether or not you achieve your goals. The company you keep defines who you are, and if you want to become a more focused person, you can no longer afford to surround yourself with people who will be counterproductive to your efforts. For example, if your goal was to give up eating chocolate for a year until you reach your fitness goal, it wouldn't help if you were surrounded by friends who were constantly snacking on chocolate. The temptation will eventually be too much for you to resist, and you'll fall off the wagon before you've reached your finishing goal. This is not a good way to stay motivated. Unfortunately, the truth is that some people, even the people who are currently important in your life right now, are simply no good for you. These individuals who are the opposite of what success should be will only serve to drain the energy out of you and fill your life, and your thoughts, with negativity. This is something you do not have the luxury of anymore, from this point on. Even if they are friends whom you may have known your entire life, just one bad apple in the bunch is enough to spoil the entire basket. What this means is that, even if you have even one negative person in your life, it can do catastrophic and disastrous damage to all the effort you have put thus far towards bettering yourself. Instead, you should be spending your time with people who have the same goal or people who have already achieved that goal. The latter will serve as an inspiration for you to keep going.

- **Do You Have the Little Milestones That Keep You Incentivized Daily?** - To stick to your goals and keep diligently working on it daily until it happens, you need to feel inspired by those goals. When it feels like your goal is still far away from being accomplished, it can put a damper on your motivation. This is why you need to have little milestones that keep you motivated daily. These little milestones are the small changes that you can see taking place daily. When you work on your goals each day, make a note of the progress you've made. Every effort that you put it, no matter how small, is still one step better than you were yesterday. That is a milestone you should be proud of. Every little change helps. You should be keeping track of every progress that you make. Whenever you feel dejected or demotivated, pick up your little notebook and take a look at how far you have come since you first started. They say that a goal without a plan is nothing more than a wish. Tony Robbins once said, *"Setting goals is the first step you need to take the invisible and make it visible."* Write your goals down because this makes your progress a focus point. When you clearly see what is taking place, it keeps you accountable. You will automatically start doing things to make sure that you are aligned with your goals. What you are trying to do here is ensure that what you want, what you say, what you do, and what you think about are all aligned with your goals. This is how to turn them into reality.

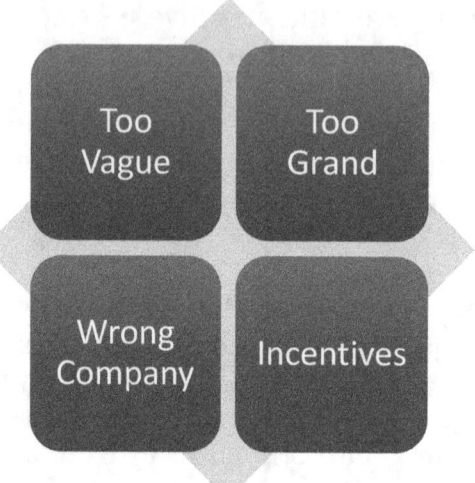

Goal-Setting Mistakes to Avoid

To ensure the goals you set are effective, and you achieve the desired outcome you want, you need to avoid the most common goal-setting mistakes that many people make.

- **Mistake #1: They Don't Have the Big Picture In Mind** - The first mistake that many people make is that they don't have a clear vision for their life. They don't know what the big picture is because they have never given it some serious thought. They are not clear about what it is that they truly want, and they don't know what they are moving towards. Goals are stepping stones, and they are specific results, actions, or things that you need to achieve to bring you close to your ultimate vision. A lot of people make the mistake of not thinking enough about the long-term. They don't think about the big picture. What a lot of people do is only think about five years from now or ten years from now. You should be thinking about your entire life and what you want it to be, and every small, digestible goal that you set from this point on should act as the building block that will lead you to that final destination. Always start with the end in mind. Look at the big picture of what you are setting your goals for, and make sure that all your goals are in alignment with that big picture thinking. Don't forget that the purpose of setting a goal is to create the ideal life you want for yourself and the person that you want to become.

- **Mistake #2 - Your Goals Are Unattainable -** There is a trick to making goals work. What you should do is create goals that seem unattainable at the moment for the short-term but possible with the big picture approach. For example, if you're making minimum wage right now, setting a goal to achieve a million dollars in a year is not realistic. You are setting yourself up to fail. However, making a million dollars in five, perhaps ten years from now, is entirely possible, and the short-term goals that you create will be responsible for leading you there. Your goals should be the sweet spot between pushing you out of your comfort zone, yet still, something that you know for a fact you can achieve within the timeframe that you set for yourself. *That is an attainable goal.* When you set a goal for yourself, you should rate that goal on a scale of one to ten. Ask yourself on a scale of one to ten how much desire do you have to achieve that goal? How motivated are you to follow through and achieve this goal within the timeframe you set for yourself? That is the secret to setting attainable goals. This is what we call the "sweet spot" goals. Ideally, your goals should have you on a scale of seven and above. Anything less than seven, and you're not going to be as motivated as you think you will achieve that goal after all. Maybe you will be pumped up and excited in the beginning, but that will quickly fade away if you don't want it badly enough. The second piece of the puzzle to avoid this mistake is that you have to *believe* you can achieve the goal. Desire alone is not going to be enough. You need to believe that you have it in you to achieve this goal. Otherwise, you're going to doubt yourself every step of the way. No matter what goal you set for yourself, you *must be able to follow through*. Avoid setting goals that are too hard and too challenging right away because you're only setting yourself up for failure if you do this.

- **Mistake #3: You Don't Know Your Reason for Setting That Goal In the First Place -** This is another common mistake that gets made during the goal-setting process. Most people are so eager to set goals for the sake of being able to say that they have set a goal. They don't stop to think about the reason *why* they are choosing that particular goal in the first place. They don't think about the reason *why* they set this goal for themselves. Oh, yes, you can have a goal. But you also need to know the reason *why* you want this goal to happen. Your reason is going to be the key point that your mind focuses on when you struggle. When you're on the verge of quitting and wanting to give up, concentrating on the reason why you wanted to start in the first place will give you the drive to keep ongoing. The reasons that you have are the fuel for your fire. When you are very clear about why you're doing something, it gives you focus and clarity. It makes you feel even more passionate about your goals because there is a sense of purpose there. How often have you stopped to ask yourself why you're doing this? When you ask yourself the question of why you are setting these goals, are you able to answer it definitively? The reasons are the difference between those who succeed in their goals and those who fail. Without that extra push, that necessary kick in the butt, many of us would be guilty of slacking off far too much and taking things easy. Your reason why is going to be the reason you find the desire to stay motivated to improve your life. Motivation is the driving force that will fuel you to take action, even when you're reluctant and don't want to do it because it's hard. The mark of a truly successful person is when they dig deep and find that willpower to do the things they don't want to do. The trouble with a lot of people who fail is that they set goals, but they don't want them badly enough. This is like the eighty-something percent of the Harvard group who did not make any goals at all and the ones who made the goals but did not commit to them on paper. You have to make sure that you are excited about your goals. More importantly, you have to make sure you know the reason *why* you're setting this goal in the first place. When you get in your car, you know why you're turning the engine on and where you want to go. You don't get in your car without a clue and drive aimlessly around. The same thing can be said about your goals. Avoid setting a goal for the sake of being able to say that you've set a goal. Set a goal with a purpose and a reason why. The questions you need to ask yourself are: *Why must I achieve this goal? What are the consequences if you don't achieve this goal? Why is this goal worth sacrificing and pushing yourself beyond your comfort zone?*

- **Mistake #4: You Don't Have A Plan** - Remember how a goal without a plan is nothing more than a wish. Well, this is going to explain why. Your goal is a target. If you're in a car or an airplane, your goal would be your destination. To get to that destination, you need actions, strategies, and tasks that need to be accomplished before you can say that you made it. For example, let's say that you wanted to go to Bali for a holiday. That is your destination (goal). You want to be in Bali. Now that you know where you want to be, the question is, *how do you get there?* Your plan of action is going to be scouring the Internet for the next few weeks until you land at the best possible price for a plane ticket. Your next plan of action is going to be to get your travel documents in order and also book a hotel, securing yourself a place to stay when you arrive. The third plan of action would be to pack your bags and make a checklist to ensure you have everything you need. Finally, all that is left is to get on that plane, fly to your destination, and have fun. Do you see why having a plan matters? Without a plan, all you would do is say you want to go to Bali for a holiday, and that would be in. Nothing would get booked, no travel arrangements made, and in the end, the holiday doesn't happen. With goals, what you should do is to engineer them backward. You want to commit that goal to paper, and then work your way backward by breaking that goal down into smaller chunks. Like the Bali holiday example. You could also create a list of what you *could do* along with a list of what you should do. This means that you have a list of all the things that you should be doing, but you have a second list of additional steps you *could* do to make those goals happen faster. The best way to get inspiration for the things you should and could do would be to look at others who have achieved similar goals. Find inspiration from their stories, and look at the steps that they took to make their goal happen. What did they make it a point to concentrate on? What action steps did you take that yielded the most result? When you find a proven plan that someone else has already done successfully, this only cements in your mind that if they could do it, you can do it too.

- **Mistake #5: You Don't Take Action** - Without action, you cannot achieve the results you want. It is as simple as that. You need to develop a consistent habit of following up on your goals. Goals involve plans, and these plans are going to require you to commit to them until you see the fruits of your labor. You need to consistently follow up on your goals to assess where you are at. You need to set goals because it helps you overcome any procrastination tendencies you may have. When you've got goals and an action plan to work on, you become accountable for your own success, and that makes it very real. You know from this point on that your success depends entirely on you and the effort that you put into today, tomorrow, next week, and every week until your goal are accomplished. These goals help remind you to stay motivated and to stay on track because it gives you something to work for. Goals are a great start and a great way to move forward with your plans. A goal can change your life because it gives you the laser-sharp focus that you need, and taking action consistently every step of the way is how to keep that ability to concentrate and motivation burning strong. When you are conducting a review of your goals, go through each of the steps you took, and evaluate how well you did. Were you on track? Did things progress the way that you hoped it would? Do you need to do anything differently at the next step? You need to take an honest look at your progress and evaluate what needs to be changed. *That is taking action.* Another way to take action is to make your goal-setting process a commitment to yourself. When you set a goal, make a commitment to yourself that you are going to see it through to the end. Make it a promise to yourself. Think of each goal, similar to a contract between you and your dream life. Contracts are binding, and so should your commitment to your goal be. Every action that you take, even if it is a small one, should bring you one step closer to your goal. Every day brings you a little bit further, so never allow yourself to get discouraged by the setbacks you encounter. Challenges are a part of this package, there is no one out there who doesn't face a challenge or two. This is why evaluating your goals at frequent intervals is an important action to take, because it will tell you if you were off track. This will enable you to make the necessary adjustments when you have a working process of always checking in on your goals. That is taking action.

Goals are a confidence-building exercise. Think of your goals as a target. You have a bow and arrow in your hand, and each time you hit the target's bullseye, your confidence increases, and so does your happiness. You can't help but feel pleased with yourself for hitting that goal, and that fuels your belief in yourself that you can do it again. This is why it is important to set achievable goals. By hitting the target each time, your confidence and your belief in yourself strengths, and this will encourage and motivate you to keep on pushing forward, even when you are faced with setbacks because you know that you can do this. You have to become someone who is committed to finishing what they started. This is the only way to enhance your ability to concentrate and keep you on the right track for success. If the goals aren't working, then change the goals to become something that you want so badly you will be willing to do anything for it. If you need a reason and a focal point to concentrate on, let it be your goals since the goals are going to be the one that turns our life around.

Chapter 3

Prioritizing Productive Habits and Schedules

Aristotle once said that we are what we repeatedly do. He believed that excellence was a habit that we cultivated, not a single act alone. It takes a lot of willpower to remain productive from the time you wake up in the morning, and it takes even more willpower to keep those positive habits going. To boost your powers of focus, what you need to develop are the right kind of habits, and these should be habits that encourage you to prioritize your productivity.

What Are Habits?
Habits contribute to a large part of our lifestyle. Most of the things that we do each day are done out of habit. For example, brushing our teeth, taking a shower, commuting to work, responding to emails, scrolling through social media. A habit is something that you do every single day, and you do it without thinking. You go through the motions on auto-pilot because you have become so accustomed to the routine that you don't think about it anymore. Habits are responsible for shaping our lives, whether we realize it or not. What you do consistently on a daily basis is either going to be beneficial or

destructive to your life. There is power in this simple piece of information. When you know that your habits can make or break you, you also know that you can choose to change the habits that have shaped your life thus far and replace them with better habits. For example, once you identify the habits that have been holding you back and made it difficult for you to concentrate, then you know that you need to replace these habits if you want to see any kind of positive change.

Creating new habits is something that takes time, patience, and, most importantly, persistence. There is a reason why productive and focused people get more things done in a day. It is because they are practicing certain habits which you are not. They have found and developed productivity habits which work for them, they have trained themselves to have the needed discipline to stick to those habits, and they have made it a part of their lifestyle until productivity now becomes second nature to them. If becoming a more productive person at the end of this book is your ultimate goal, then there's only one thing you need to do. Start practicing these habits too, just like what they're doing. The great thing about these habits is they're not impossible to adopt, and just about everyone can do it, all you need is the want and the desire to make the change and become a better you. It is not going to be easy breaking out of your old routine. It is going to feel strange at first, mostly because you're not used to it. The question you need to ask yourself now is, *"What are some of the ideal habits I should add into my life and why?"*.

The Current Habits That Are Killing Your Productivity

You probably know about the obvious productivity killers. A noisy environment, mobile devices (it goes without saying), the temptation to do anything else but work. But what about the less than obvious killers that are silently causing problems you're not aware of?

- **You're Afraid to Work Hard -** Yes, some people are afraid to work hard because it requires *too much effort*. It's much easier to make excuses as to why you *can't* do something rather than muster up your energy and internal motivation to sit down and finish what you set out to do. Winners are not afraid of buckling down and working hard because they know that any success worth achieving in life is going to have to be earned. That determination and commitment to working hard are what got these winners to a successful point in their lives, and that is what you need to start doing right now. Unfortunately, we happen to be living in a generation of shortcuts, quick-fixes, and instant answers and replies. We have forgotten what it is like to work hard for something, especially when it comes to the younger generation. However, if you truly want to become someone who is more productive, you must never back down from a challenge and never be afraid to work hard for what you want. You may struggle, you may cry, you may take one step forward and two steps back. But if Thomas Edison had quit when he failed at making the lightbulb the first one thousand times, where would we be today?

- **You're Striving for Perfectionism -** Perfectionism is a concept that does not exist, and it is time to put it out of your mind. Nobody is ever perfect, at least, not completely. Nothing can ever be done perfectly all the time. Perfectionism only leads to excuses and not getting anything done. A perfectionist has strong beliefs about how their work or project should look. The perfectionist is frozen by their inability to achieve their own lofty standard. You'll find excuses why you shouldn't get started yet, why it is not ready because you find things to keep tweaking again and again. There will always be one flaw or another in everything that you do. By focusing on perfectionism, you could tinker on a task for months without getting anything done. The perfectionist in you is killing your productivity, and it is time that it stopped. Perfectionists can set unreachable goals for themselves sometimes, and then it hits them hard if they fail to accomplish those goals because of that high level of expectation they set for themselves. Aiming too high, especially when the expectations are unrealistic, is a surefire way to set yourself up for failure. When you spend far too much time planning for perfection, you come up with all sorts of excuses to procrastinate and delay your plan because it will never be perfect enough to be executed in time. According to some psychologists, the antidote is to question one's beliefs and replace them with rational ones. If you are a perfectionist unable to start a project, you can question yourself.

- **You're Trying to Do Everything Yourself -** While you do need to have a to-do list to keep you structured and organized, having a to-do list that is twenty or thirty items too long is too much. A to-do list should only consist of the most important items that will either make a difference in your day or move you one step closer to your big picture goals. That is it, that is all your list should consist of, nothing more. You can't rank every single item on your to-do list with the same priority because you are only setting yourself up for failure. We only have a limited amount of time and resources we can commit daily to getting work-related tasks done since we have other responsibilities that need attending to as well. There is no way you can complete thirty or forty to-do items a day, and by sticking to this habit, you're only going to feel demotivated at the end of each day when your to-do list still seems like a mile long. The successful, productive people can get more done in a day with the same twenty-four hours everyone has because they are very clear about where their time deserves to be spent. Sometimes, you need to know when to ask for help.

- **Forgetting That You Can Burn Out** - We are not robots, and we will eventually burn out if we keep pushing too hard. Some people become so focused on checking and crossing things off their list that they forget to take a break. The problem is that even though you want to be as productive as you can be, the human brain is a cognitive miser. We also don't run on an unlimited supply of energy. If you are someone who feels a surge of energy at the start of the day only to have the energy dwindle by the time late afternoon rolls around, you might be trying to do too much without giving yourself enough breaks to recharge your batteries. Managing your time better doesn't mean working for eight hours straight like a machine powering through all your tasks. Not taking breaks when required is how you burn out quickly, and that then becomes counterproductive because when you're burned out, it becomes harder to get back into focus, and you lose time doing it. Whenever you've completed a task on your to-do list, and you feel like you need a quick breather, go ahead and take it. Take a break, recharge, refocus your energy, and then come back with renewed vigor to tackle the next task before you. We are cognitive misers, and this means that we have limited willpower and limited cognitive powers to expand at any given time. Doing too much without giving yourself enough time to recharge is one of the reasons why you struggle to maintain your ability to concentrate at optimum levels after a while.

- **You're Not Allocating Enough Time Per Task** - When you know that you have a lot to do per day, it can be tempting to try and cram everything in and rush through each task. Another common pitfall that leads to a lot of stress and a loss of your ability to concentrate is when you miscalculate the time and effort you are going to need to complete a particular task. The absence of realistic timelines is a habitual mistake that leads to a lot of unnecessary stress when you're scrambling at the last minute as you realize you're running out of time. What you should be doing instead is analyzing each task that you have in front of you and then set a realistic time frame for how long you would need to complete it. Don't set a timeline that you think should be the right one. Instead, look at the task objectively and realistically decide how much time should be allocated to this task depending on how much work is going to be involved or how complicated the task is.

- **You Think You Need to Be Productive *All The Time*** - This is another common mistake and assumption that a lot of people make about productivity. Your work and your life are blending together because you don't know how to separate them anymore. Not when emails keep buzzing in on your phone throughout the day and well into the night when you should be done with work for the day. Unbeknownst to you, this is subconsciously causing you a great deal of stress, and when you are stressed, it becomes much harder to remain productive. This bad habit of believing that we need to be busy all the time has also led to another equally bad habit called multitasking. We have been told that multitasking is helpful in getting things done. Your internet browser probably has multiple tabs open at any given time, and your phone is most likely beside you and interrupting at intervals even as you read this. This has become the norm, and it has become a way of life for many, but that does not mean that it is the *right* way of life. Have you ever tried to text and drive at the same time? There is a reason it is dangerous. Doing multiple things at once means that nothing gets done well or efficiently. Learn to do one thing at a time and always carry it to completion. Do not start another task until the first has been completed. Multitasking is only killing your productivity silently while you continue to labor under the false assumption that you're "getting more done" by multitasking.

- **You're Focused on Too Many Apps and Hacks -** Along with the false sense of belief that we need to multitask, most people also seem to be on a never-ending quest to find the latest app, hack, trick, or tool that they hope is going to boost their productivity levels. In the end, your phone could be filled with at least ten apps you downloaded, hoping that it would make a difference. But if you are honest with yourself, how many of these apps do you actually use? If you acknowledged the truth, it is not the apps that will make a difference to your productivity levels. That kind of change needs to come from within, and this is one of the many reasons why you are reading this. If all the apps, hacks, tricks, and tools worked, almost everyone out there would be incredible workhorses with productivity levels that never seem to fade. Apps don't work because it does not address the underlying challenges we face, no matter how great that app is or what amazing features it holds. Having multiple apps is a distraction because it is going to be confusing, not knowing where to start or what you should be focused on. Now, that is not to say that the tools are not helpful, because they can be useful. The tools matter, but they don't matter as much as we think that they do. Put away your productivity tools temporarily and go back to the fundamentals. The good old pen and paper.

- **You Believe that Being Busy Is the Same As Being Productive -** Having a long to-do list in front of you may lead you to believe that you're "busy being productive." However, if that actually worked, you wouldn't have those moments at the end of the day where you feel like you've done nothing, even though you felt busy. That is because being busy is *not the same* as being productive. Being busy is causing a lack of direction. When you have twenty or thirty tasks competing for your attention, and your focus is pulled in twenty or thirty different ways. You're losing sight of your goals. The more distracted you become, the further you slip from your goals as you keep getting sidetracked by menial tasks that neither make you happy, more productive, or contribute in any significant way to your happiness. In fact, the only thing that's happening here is that you continue to keep yourself in the cycle of wasting time. This is a very chronic problem in a world of information overload.

How to Break Out of Old Habits

The first thing you need to do is identify all the old habits that have made it difficult for you to concentrate in the past. You would then pick one habit and start small by concentrating on changing that habit first. Pick the habit that will make the biggest difference to start with. For example, if your habit of scrolling through social media for hours has been the biggest stumbling block in your ability to concentrate, then pick that as the first habit you want to work on. What you are trying to do is build up your new habits slowly, rather than try to tackle everything at once. Slow and steady is the strategy that wins the race at the end of the day. When you take things slowly and do it one and a time, it will feel a lot more manageable. Start by practicing your new habits once or twice a week, even if that doesn't feel like a lot. The little changes will make a big difference.

Once or twice a week, commit to turning your phone off, putting it away in a drawer, and then working steadily on a task of your choice for the day. Keep working, and don't stop to pick up your phone until it is done. Once you've finished, you can reward yourself with a little bit of social media time, but not until the work is done. If you do it this way, you break out of your old habit of being distracted by social media slowly but surely. Start small by doing it once or twice a week until you gradually build up to doing it daily. You might feel tempted to be ambitious and try to tackle ten or fifteen positive habits in a day, but avoid overwhelming yourself. You want to be able to stick to your new habit routine, not feel so put off by it that you give up and go back to your old ways because it feels easier to do that.

- **Identify What Triggers Your Bad Habits** - Do you know the reason behind your procrastination tendencies? What makes it difficult for you to concentrate? Psychologists believe that being able to identify your triggers will make it much easier for you to come up with solutions to overcome them. If you find it difficult to stay focused and concentrate, there must be a reason for it. There is always a trigger. Examples of these triggers include a noisy environment, a lack of motivation, too many factors demanding your attention at the same time. There is always a trigger for your behavior, and you need to identify what these triggers are before you can come up with the steps to break these bad habits.

- **Don't Reject the Obstacles** - It is important that you make peace with the fact that this journey is going to be hard. Overcoming your old habits is going to be tough for a lot of people, and you need to embrace the difficulty. If you don't, your subconscious mind is always going to reject the process. You will find it difficult to initiate any kind of change when your brain keeps telling you this is not worth it or that it is too much effort. It is not going to be all rainbows and butterflies. A lot of people find it difficult to stick to the goals and commitments they make because they don't view the obstacles in front of them seriously. When you don't take a realistic view of the challenges that are going to come, it will be very easy to feel discouraged and unmotivated when the challenge does hit you in the face. To avoid being disillusioned as you try to overcome your bad habits, make a list of all the possible obstacles you anticipate and prepare another list of all the ways you can overcome them. In other words, you should always aim to have backup plans to keep you from sliding back into your old habits. As important as it is to break out of your old bad habits, it is equally important to embrace the fact that failure is going to be part of the process.

- **Create A Reward System for Yourself** - Breaking bad habits is going to be hard work, and like your goals, you need to find ways to keep yourself incentivized throughout the process. At least, until the new habit you're trying to create becomes a routine. Creating a reward system gives your mind something else to think about besides how difficult this process is. Giving yourself a well-earned treat or break after a long week of working hard on your new habit gives your brain something to look forward to. Since the human brain is wired for pleasure, a reward system could be just what you need to keep you motivated long enough to make the habit stick permanently.

- **Don't Quit When You Experience Failure** - Remember that failure is part of the process of breaking habits. If all the successful people in the world failed when things got tough or when they experienced a failure, they would never have made it as far as they did. You will stumble and fall probably several times along the way, but the most important thing is to never give up. We have a tendency to be too hard on ourselves whenever we make a mistake. Instead of seeing mistakes as failures, see them as learning lessons instead. You are stronger than your temptations, and that is something you need to always remind yourself of.

Building Better Habits for Greater Productivity

It is no secret that some of the most successful people in the world have a work schedule that, you might say, is insane.

Take Elon Musk, for example, who probably works more than double the hours of the average employee. What is even more incredible is that he splits his time and focus in between several different projects, *but* he can still give a hundred percent of his ability to concentrate and effort for each of these projects. How does he do it? What habits do Musk, and many of his successful peers have that the rest of us are missing out on? How do they concentrate so well when the rest of us seem to struggle just to fight off the distraction factors?

The answer lies in the productive habits, and schedule individuals like Musk have built for themselves. They never let distractions control them. Distractions are everywhere, but productive people have mastered the art of learning how to tune them out and not letting it bother them. They're able to completely remove distractions from their frame of mind, especially if there's an important task that needs to be attended to. If you want to be productive, you're going to have to do the same and remove all causes for temptation when you need to buckle down and get something done. The answer lies in the way that you structure your day to make it more productive and successful. The reason you find it difficult sometimes to plow through a task is that the current system which you have is probably not working well for you. If that is the case, then it's time to copy what the productive people do and create your own work system which works for you. Find a way or a system that makes you feel more motivated, and mold it to your current work habits.

- **Plan Your Day Meticulously** - Details are going to be your best friend as you work on trying to master your ability to concentrate based on the necessary skills. Every minute that you spend planning and structuring your day will save you *ten minutes* in terms of execution time. Planning your day is one of the most productive habits you can build for yourself, and ideally, you want to start planning your day the night before. Take a pen and paper, sit down, and write down everything you have to do the next day. Next to each task, write the amount of time you need to allocate to concentrate on each task. Structuring and planning your day should be the last thing that you do at the end of each day. If you don't fancy doing it the night before, then make it the first thing that you do every morning. Before you check your phone, messages, texts, emails, notifications, and before anything else, wake up, plan, and structure your entire day. Make a list of everything that you have to do that day, along with the time allocated for each task. Having a list will give you a structure to work with for your entire day, and for some people, the structure is the best thing they can do for their productivity levels. When you start working from a list, you will increase both your productivity and your output by at least twenty-five percent. When your productivity levels increase, your ability to concentrate is automatically growing along with it. All successful people work from lists, and this is what you need to do too.

- **Set Priorities for Your List -** Another way to create some structure to your day and make it more productive is to set a priority order to your list. Productive people very rarely just go with the flow. Instead, they prefer to be organized and plan a list of things that they need to get done for the day, the week, or even the month. It's how they stay on track towards achieving the goals they set for themselves, and how it is that they always seem to get more stuff done than those of you who are, say, not as productive as you should be. Once you've written down everything you need to do, look through the list, and apply the *80/20 Rule*. Based on this rule, if you have ten items on your list, then two of those items are going to be more valuable than the other eight put together. This means that you should aim to work on the two most important tasks first before you attempt to tackle anything else that is on your list.

- **Apply the Five Second Rule -** When you're about to carry out your new habit, do it in five seconds, and don't give yourself too much time to think about it. What you are aiming to do is physically take action on your habit without thinking too much about it. If you think about it too much, you could end up talking yourself out of it, and this is something you want to avoid. If you start taking action without thinking about it, then you are less likely to talk yourself out of it. Get to your action within five seconds, and that is how you do it.

- **You Need to Know When You Should Outsource -** Knowing when to ask for help and the tasks that you are better off outsourcing can be one of the most productive things you do for yourself. Tim Ferris talks about this in his famous *Four Hour Work Week*. The idea is to pick one thing you can outsource each week that will save you one hour. It could be tasks that are as simple as getting someone else to do your laundry or go grocery shopping for you. If you have the resources to outsource a task that is going to free up more time to do something productive, why not do it?

- **Make Your New Habit Easy and Convenient -** Your new habit should be easy and convenient enough to execute without too much effort on your part. If something involves too much work, you're less likely to stick to it long-term because of the hassle involved. For example, your new habit of putting turning off your phone and tucking it away in your drawer where it is going to be out of sight is easy enough to carry out. It doesn't require too much effort on your part, and you can complete the action within a matter of seconds. Therefore, you're a lot more likely to make this a habit each time you need to buckle down and concentrate on getting some work done. If your new habit is to drink more water, then placing a water bottle on your desk at all times is how you make this habit easy and convenient to carry out.

- **Be Consistent Before You Scale -** You want to be as consistent as possible with your new habit before you aim to scale and build on that habit. For example, let's say that the habit you are trying to build is to work for an hour on any given task before you pay attention to anything else. You want to make this a consistent practice before you aim to increase that duration to two hours, three hours, or four. There is a simple explanation for this, and that reason is that you are trying to build enough discipline to stay focused enough before you try to push yourself to do better. To master this habit, you would need to become a master of self-discipline. You see, self-discipline is not easy either, and you know by now that doing too much too soon is never the way to go. It is about striking a balance, knowing when you should resist temptation, and controlling the urge to always give in to your desires. The temptation is always going to be there, and you want to make sure you're the master of level one before you scale all the way up to level two.

- **You Need to Visualize and Be Committed -** When productive people set a goal for themselves, they're not just setting a goal. They're making a commitment to seeing it through. This is a habit they have created for themselves. This commitment helps them to stay productive because they don't care how long it takes or how hard they have to work, as long as they get the results that they want in the end. They have also trained themselves to consistently visualize the end goal they have in mind. Right from the beginning, people who are productive know what they want. They know what they are doing, why they're doing it, and what needs to be done. They can visualize and see it crystal clear in their mind, and this is a habit that you need to start cultivating for yourself too.

- **Give Yourself a Purpose Each Day** - Every change begins in your mind. A shift in the mindset can bring about the biggest lifestyle changes, and all it takes is a slight difference in the way that you think about something or say something. For instance, if you give yourself a purpose each day and say, *"I am the kind of person who can concentrate for more than an hour on a task I have to do,"* you're already changing your perception about your ability to concentrate. A productive person gets out of bed each morning with a purpose. They tell themselves all the things they are going to accomplish during the day, and they don't waste any time getting started. Even if the goal or the task at hand may be something small, training themselves to wake up each day with a purpose and the intention to get things done is what helps train them to get into a productive mindset and way of thinking. The idea is to step into the mindset, and the behavior will eventually follow.

It's going to take some getting used to, and the initial adjustment could be difficult for many, especially when you're not used to being productive. It's going to feel weird in the beginning, and there'll probably be several times when you're tempted to give in to the urge to just quit, but don't. Don't do it. If you can push through the initial difficult phase in the beginning, it will all be worth it, and it only gets better from there. The American philosopher and psychologist William James once said that *one of the most important discoveries of this century is the discovery that man can change his circumstance by changing his attitude.* A change of attitude is needed for self-improvement and better productivity because you cannot expect big changes without putting in the work for it. Having a more productive outlook is the first step towards turning your life around, and when you change your attitude, it becomes much easier to change everything else, including adopting new habits that will make you a much more productive person. Soon, these habits will become so much a part of your routine that you don't even feel it anymore, and it comes naturally to you without a second thought.

Chapter 4

Turbocharge Your Focus with the Targeted Approach to Overcoming Procrastination

To supercharge your ability to concentrate, you need to overcome the number one barrier that stands in front of everyone and their quest for better focus. That barrier is none other than the dreaded *procrastination.*

Understanding Your Procrastination Tendencies

We know procrastination is a terrible habit we are all guilty of. Yet, *why do we do it?* Why do we keep repeating this behavior when we know that it is not going to do us any favors? Procrastination is an irrational decision to delay doing something. If we look at most forms of procrastination closely, we will realize that it is a choice for instant gratification over future rewards or suffering. Sometimes the urge to put off something unpleasant can be too strong to ignore any longer. After all, if something is unpleasant, we automatically have no motivation to get it done, right? We know that eventually, we are going to have to bite the bullet and do it anyway, yet we still continue to give in to the desire to procrastinate. Now, procrastination is a habit that is more complex. It is much more than bad time management or laziness. Several subfields of psychology even have a different way of looking at procrastination. For example, a neuropsychologist would refer to procrastination as a *"failure of executive function."* In other words, those who procrastinate fail when it comes to their ability to plan ahead or prioritize. Those who procrastinate are unable to say, *"I am going to do this and stick to it."* Instead, what tends to happen is one person might sit down to get started on a task but take ages gathering the material and resources they need. Someone else might attempt to start a task but get stuck at different points throughout the process until they finally end up neglecting the task altogether. This is why it is called a failure of executive function. That is just the point of view of the neuropsychologist.

A social psychologist, on the other hand, would view procrastination as a problem that relates to emotional regulation. From the social psychologists' point of view, people tend to procrastinate to avoid bad feelings like stress and disappointment. One psychologist named Timothy Pychyl says that procrastination is *"giving in to feel good."* Procrastination makes you want to cash in on the short-term, feel-good feeling you get by putting off work and relaxing for a bit, even though you know you're going to pay for it later. The more unpleasant the task is, the higher the tendency to procrastinate. For example, when you don't want to write a big essay because you're feeling tired, and you tell yourself you'll do it later when you feel better. Sure, there is nothing wrong with that, but researchers like Pychyl point out when you do this all the time, *then* it becomes a problem. Habitually putting off tasks to push away those bad feelings is going to come back to haunt you eventually. Evolutionary psychologists, however, see procrastination as a problem that could be related genetic. Despite the different points of view and study approaches to the subject, the one thing all psychologists can agree on is that procrastination will never bring you any good.

Procrastination has been around for a long time. There was once a Greek poet named Hesiod who wrote about this bad habit in 700BCE. In his writings, Hesiod said this: *Do not put off your work until tomorrow or the day after, for the sluggish worker does not fill his barn. The industry makes work go well, but a man who puts off work is always at handgrips with ruin."* Procrastination has become an epidemic because it is simply too hard to resist. Our motivation is affected by four key factors:

- Our confidence and belief in our ability to succeed.
- We have the adequate time needed to complete the tasks.
- You need to have the right incentives to keep us motivated.
- The impulsivity factor.

When one or more of these factors are lacking at any given time, we lose our desire to stay on task.

You might say that we are living in an era where procrastination has become an epidemic. No, that is not an exaggeration, especially given the fact that more people struggle with procrastination today compared to any other period throughout history. Why has this tendency to put off the tasks we don't want to do escalated to the point where it has become an epidemic? There are several reasons for that:

- **It Could Be Blamed on Genetics -** Some studies show that there is a possibility procrastination is a tendency that is inherited. It could be a product of evolution, like what evolutionary psychologists believe. Apparently, it is a trait that has evolved to keep us from making rash and impulsive decisions. In that sense, you might say that procrastinating on certain things might be somewhat beneficial. This would depend on the context of the situation, of course. Researchers at the University of Colorado, Boulder, conducted a study in 2014 where they tried to determine if procrastination had a genetic component to it. To figure this out, researchers studied pairs of twins and asked them about their work habits. Researchers compared fraternal twins (twins who only share some of their DNA) and identical twins (twins who share all their DNA). Each set of these twins grew up together with the same environmental influences, and thus, researching their responses would help to determine if procrastination was somehow tied to genetics. The researchers in this study came up with a mathematical model to help them calculate if procrastination could be inherited. What they found out was that half the time, the differences in procrastination habits could be attributed to differences in genetics. This happens to be the case with a lot of inherited behavioral traits. Some variations are bound to occur due to environmental factors. Findings from other studies revealed that variations in procrastination habits were also linked to genetic variations in another trait. That trait is impulsivity. Therefore, the researchers concluded that putting things off and behaving impulsively, are behaviors that could be inherited together. Coincidentally, these traits are also related to goal-management.

- **We're Faced with *Too Many Options* -** In the days when our ancestors had to hunt for food, procrastination would only lead to one outcome. That outcome was starvation. If they procrastinated on their responsibilities to hunt for food, then they would have to go without food. These days, procrastination doesn't have such dire consequences. Turning in a report late at work is not going to be as disastrous as having to go without food or starving through the night. Therefore, we have the luxury of slacking off a little bit, and we know it. Procrastination is such a major obstacle to overcome today because there is no sense of urgency. The consequences are not dramatic enough to warrant immediate action from us, thus, we have no push to get things done. In fact, being faced with too many choices actually leads to some people being *afraid* of making any choice at all. When you become too scared to make any kind of decision, that leads to procrastination too. In theory, the power of choice sounds like it should be easy enough, but it may not always be quite that simple. The knowledge that you have a big decision to make can be daunting, especially when the consequences of that choice rests on your shoulders. Whether that decision turns out to be for the best or otherwise, you had the power to make that happen. The pressure to make the right choice can cause anxiety in some people, and this is when they find themselves stuck in a rut and unable to move forward because they're too afraid of making the wrong choice. Rather than endure all the possible risks of things going wrong, it seems a lot easier to procrastinate instead.

- **Having Fun Is Much Easier** - Thinking requires a lot of energy. The part of the brain that you need to engage to carry out those decision-making choices requires a lot of energy. Having fun requires considerably less energy, and that is why it always seems easier to scroll through social media instead of finishing that report you're supposed to be working on. It's much easier to scroll through Facebook than it is to get through the mountain of paperwork on your desk that is waiting for you. It is certainly easier to find excuses *not* to do something too. Procrastinating and finding excuses is much easier than slogging through a task that you're dreading. Being hardworking and committed to meeting goals is the one that is difficult because it requires willpower and discipline, two qualities that you need to have about you if you hope to achieve success. Procrastinating, a lack of self-discipline and willpower will prove to be a hindrance because the level of success you achieve is going to boil down to your attitude at the end of the day. If you spend most of your time just wasting time, then expect that the results you are going to get are going to be along those lines.

- **We Live in A World That Is Fast-Paced and Distracting -** We live in a world that is fast-paced and full of distractions. The lifestyles we lead today can be immensely overwhelming. Not everyone enjoys being busy and on the move all the time, with no time to stop and take a break for themselves. Procrastination is almost like a way of rebelling against the system. Not only is the world we live in fast-paced, but it also happens to be very distracting. Mobile phones, laptops, tablets, and the Internet are literally everywhere you go. With access to the worldwide web anytime we need, procrastination is becoming a temptation that is too hard to resist. If you think about it, most of the time that you spend on the internet is spent procrastinating. We lose a lot of productivity by checking emails and scrolling through social media.

- **You Carry A Negative Mindset With You -** Sometimes, a negative mindset can cause you to start believing that you're not good enough, or you're not deserving enough, and thus, it would be better to just not do it at all rather than to try and risk failure. Being negative is always the easier option, being positive requires a lot more effort put into it. Having a negative state of mind will only feed into your reasons to procrastinate because you'll always be able to find a hundred reasons not to do something, even though you may have one good reason why you should. If you don't give yourself enough credit and believe in yourself enough, you will never find the extra push and the drive you need to break the cycle of procrastination.

- **You're Tempted by the Instant Gratification -** Instant gratification, or pleasure-seeking, is at the root of procrastination. You become the person who scrolls Facebook instead of starting a project, and the person who endlessly daydreams are not that different. The internet surfer receives momentary pleasure by reading his or her newsfeed. The dreamer continuously thinks about grand things from the comfort of their present life, never risking the pain of failure or the effort of trying. In both examples, seeking out pleasure is the most comfortable choice in the short-term. This is the heart of almost all procrastination. In the 1960s, a scientist named Walter Mischel studied this phenomenon of instant gratification. He began a series of experiments that are now widely referred to as the Marshmallow Experiment. He was exploring the ability of children to delay gratification for future rewards. In this experiment, a group of preschoolers was shown two plates with varying quantities of marshmallows or other snacks, a small snack, and a larger snack. When the experimenter left the room, they could ring the bell immediately, thus ending the experiment, and eat the smaller snack, or they could wait fifteen minutes and receive the larger reward. It was an experiment to see how these children did when given a choice of instant gratification or a larger future reward. Interestingly enough, a follow-up experiment was also done on some of the participants when they reached middle age. Those children who were better at delaying gratification for a future reward had achieved higher test scores, reported greater self-esteem and were even in better general health than those who were tempted by instant gratification.

BOOST YOUR FOCUS

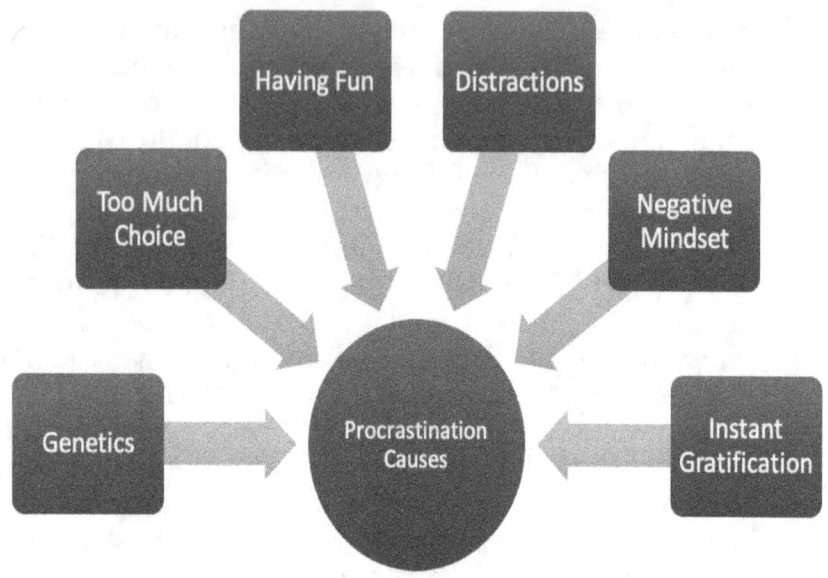

There is another interesting suggestion that researchers put forth when studying the genetic components of procrastination. They suggested that perhaps there might be an evolutionary reason why impulsive behaviors and procrastination are linked. Once again, we go back to the days of early humans. For our early ancestors to survive, they had to focus on short-term survival. They did not have time to think about their future or the long-term prospects when they didn't know if their bellies were going to be full tomorrow. Our ancestors back then were only focused on surviving day by day. When you make short-term focused and impulsive decisions proved to be a better survival technique that worked for them. However, that same approach doesn't bode so well these days. Our technology-focused world is all about long-term goals. We're encouraged to save for retirement, or plan for a vacation six months ahead, figure out a career path and where you want to be ten years from now. It is a lot of pressure for some people to handle. As it turns out, our ancestors' habit of prioritizing short-term outcomes is now encouraging us to procrastinate.

Everyone puts things off now and then, but when you start to do this habitually, your ability to concentrate at optimal levels is going to pay the price for it. There could even be a link between procrastination, depression, and anxiety. This is because people who chronically put off the things they need to do sometimes suffer from higher levels of stress. A 2015 study published in the Journal of Behavioral Medicine discovered that those who were serial procrastinators had a much harder time managing high blood pressure and heart disease. Moreover, procrastination can harm both professional and personal relationships in several ways. The most obvious way that procrastination can harm relationships is through the damage it does to our reputation and the way that others perceive us. Professionally, this can be greatly damaging. If you can only be productive when you are in a panic at the last minute, you may be viewed as disorganized, unreliable, and irresponsible, not to mention how it is going to impact your ability to stay focused and concentrate. You may be viewed as incompetent or ill-suited to your work as you struggle to maintain focus on even simple tasks. This, in turn, can affect your ability to achieve your professional goals and excel in your career.

Procrastination leads to a lot of other ripple effects that we might not have thought about along the way. For example, another big way that procrastination damages all kinds of relationships are caused by stress that is a side effect of procrastination. When you procrastinate, your mood can plummet, and irritability increases. You can become a whirlwind of negative nervous energy. This, on its own, can cause tension between friends, teammates, or lovers. When procrastinators panic in the face of the looming deadline, the task at hand can become all-consuming. Dates may be canceled, promises broken, and the procrastinator may become so absorbed in a project that he or she becomes distant. These things break trust and build resentment. An otherwise stable relationship can crack under the weight of chronic procrastination. Some procrastinators may struggle with personal relationships in a way that mystifies them. They may even find themselves seemingly unable to maintain or progress in a romantic relationship. The procrastinator may avoid even attempting to start a relationship, preferring to remain lonely rather than risk the pain of rejection.

How to Stop Procrastinating and Switch On Your Focus

The question is, what can you do to kick your focus into gear without the need for a fast-approaching deadline to really push you along? If you want to sharpen your focus so that it is strong enough to keep those procrastination urges at bay, this is what you need to do:

- **Catch the Chattering Monkey in Your Brain -** This basically means take the time to pause and notice the thoughts that are running through your mind when you're having trouble getting started on a task. These distracting thoughts that keep our mind buzzing are called the "chattering monkey" because these thoughts keep going, and they distract you from what you're supposed to do. Essentially, what you are trying to do is figure out what triggers your procrastination. To slow down your thoughts long enough to notice what is going on, you need to rely on mindfulness. The point of this is to analyze and understand the thoughts that are running through your mind. Why are you having trouble staying on task? When you do this, you should be able to pinpoint what is keeping you from staying focused. Perhaps you are feeling annoyed or frustrated at how slowly you are progressing on your project. Perhaps you're wondering what to have for dinner later. Perhaps you're fighting the temptation to binge on an entire series on Netflix right now. There is usually a distracting reason behind your procrastination, and the key is to notice what that distraction is. When you know the root cause of the problem, you can do something about it.

- **Grow A New Habit** - There are two very effective ways to create new, positive habits. The first way is to change your environment. The second is to grow that new habit *on top of an existing habit*. For example, if you were trying to get into the habit of jogging daily, you are a lot more likely to commit to this goal if your target was two hundred meters a day instead of five kilometers. The progress seems small, but the point is to work on it daily until it becomes a habit. What you can do to encourage you to concentrate is to combine two goals that you want to accomplish. For example, if you want to increase your focus *and* get fitter at the same time, you could start building the habit of doing five pushups each time you procrastinated when you should have been working. Combining procrastination with a fitness goal has an unexpected benefit to it too. The exercise is giving you a small boost in your willpower and determination, and this is going to directly impact your ability to concentrate the more you do it. If you can be disciplined enough to commit to doing five to ten pushups each time you procrastinate, you can commit to concentrating for an hour on a task that you know that you need to get done.

- **Get More Exercise Done** - Expanding on the point above, exercising can do wonders for your mental prowess. It is scientifically proven that human willpower and determination are at its highest right when we wake up and gradually lowers as the day goes on. This is why so many struggled to get to the gym after a long day in the office. When you start your day with exercise, your mental capacity for handling stress nearly triples. Our brains recognize exercise as a period of stress. As our heart rate increases, the brain kicks into a fight or flight response as a defense to the supposed threat. Our brains produce two chemicals, called Brain-Derived Neurotrophic Factor (BDNF) and endorphins. The BDNF works to protect and repair your memory neurons and acts as a reset switch, thus clearing your mind and helping you make positive decisions. Endorphins are released to minimize the discomfort of exercise, and block the sensation of pain. BDNF and endorphins are the physiological reasons exercising makes you feel so good. These chemicals are highly addictive, like morphine or heroin, or nicotine. The only difference is that they're actually good for you. BDNF is important for memory, learning, and higher thinking. By increasing your blood flow through exercise, you're getting more oxygen to the brain, and this will make it perform better. When you perform better, your willpower, and with that, your powers of focus are going to receive the much-needed boost to stay on task.

- **Separate Your Areas -** This is an important one to take note of if you're working from home. You should try to avoid mixing your areas. In other words, try not to work where you sleep and sleep where you work. It is important to keep a clear separation between work and play. Otherwise, it is going to be hard for your brain and your body to make the switch from one mode to the other. For many, creating a designated work area is key to separating work and home life. Your workspace should have a clear physical boundary, and your work should stay within that space. It should be a work area that is not susceptible to disruptions. The rest of your home can be well used for rest and relaxation and any other activities you want to get done, but in your home office area, it's all about work. The environment that you surround yourself in has a certain level of influence on our psychological state of mind. When you're stressed out by your environment, it makes it difficult to concentrate on anything. If you find it difficult to concentrate, then you know that something needs to be done. Being distracted and unable to focus on anything else except your stress is how you slowly start to burn out and feel demotivated over time. Your external physical environment can contribute to the way that you feel, and if you need more proof, just think about all those times when you were stressed out in a chaotic office environment. You want to give your brain it's best chance to stay on task by not being too distracted by your external environment. If you don't have access to a suitable area at home, choose an appropriate external site, but one where you can avoid distractions. Working in coffee shops, for example, may seem attractive, but a local library is probably a better choice. Another thing you need to do is get yourself a good workstation, make sure that you are comfortable where you are working that it is an easy, relaxed place, and you have got all the bits and pieces you need to work Don't forget that the brain cannot multitask, and therefore, it cannot make the switch quickly between work and play. Meshing those two areas together is only going to hamper your productivity and, by default, your ability to concentrate. Do yourself a favor and start designating a specific area for work if you are working from home, and if you're working at the office, avoid having lunch or taking breaks behind the desk.

- **Make Your Task List Smaller** - Making your task list smaller and a lot more achievable is going to make everything seem a lot more doable, and this is the key to tricking your brain into becoming more productive and concentrating better. When you look at an impossibly long to-do list, that is not going to motivate you. Your brain is going to feel overwhelmed, and when it does, it is going to shut down before you have even started. When we set big goals, and when we fail to accomplish them, they can be a big emotional hit for many. Feeling discouraged, we lose the drive to keep on fighting and moving forward. Eventually, it becomes easier to procrastinate because we simply don't feel like facing another possible failure yet again. As you probably know by now, this is not the best way to fuel your motivation or your focus. You need to set small goals with smaller, more doable steps to accomplish these goals. There is a special technique for this called the *Pomodoro Technique,* and this will be talked about in more detail below. This is a much better strategy because each time a goal gets smashed, seeing your goal materialize before you will help to fuel your belief that you can do this. It will make you want to do more, and eventually, your mind starts to believe you are capable of anything. When that happens, procrastination fades away and becomes a problem of the past. To overcome your tendency to procrastinate, you need to encourage your brain to think that it can complete the task that it is faced with. When your brain believes that something looks easy, you're not going to be as resistant to it. When there is no subconscious resistance, it makes it easier for you to concentrate.

- **Take Breaks Every Forty-Five Minutes -** Overcoming procrastination for better focus does not mean you should be working the right hours straight without taking a break. You're only human, not a supercomputer. In fact, it is highly recommended that you take a break every forty-five minutes to give your brain a break from all that hard work. Yes, concentrating for an extended period is hard work, and your brain is going to be fatigued if you continue to push it beyond its limits. Give yourself at least a good ten to fifteen minutes of downtime before you come back and concentrate again. When you try to push your tired brain beyond what it can do, you will find that your productivity is going to take a nosedive. Therefore, it actually pays to take breaks.

- **Reward Your Progress -** No matter how small the progress that you made, it is important to reward yourself for it. Any kind of progress is something to be proud of because it means you were better than you were yesterday. When you managed to concentrate for forty-five minutes on a task the way that you said you would, congratulate and reward yourself. You made it to your goal, and you should feel proud. If you finish your work, you can reward yourself with something you have been looking forward to. Finishing your tasks and rewarding yourself later trains your brain to believe and work towards your imagined future and that it will eventually arrive. Our brain is a highly skilled reward detector. The brain also has a pretty primitive reward system that operates on a subconscious level, and it operates on a subconscious level that was originally meant to push humans to seek out opportunities to extend their survival capacity. In today's world, however, we are all overwhelmed with many opportunities to survive from shopping to junk food, sex, drugs, and electronic gadgets. Reward yourself, even if all you did was complete two items on your task list with the ability to concentrate you wanted. That is still two items better than if you had done nothing at all. Rewarding yourself can be as simple as putting a gold star on your calendar on the days you accomplished your goals, so something more elaborate like dinner on Saturday night. This reward giving is positive reinforcement. These little things are good enough to tell your brain that you are doing something right.

Rely on the Pomodoro Technique

One of the very best ways to beat procrastination and improve your ability to concentrate is a method known as the *Pomodoro Technique*. It is a favorite technique used by many successful individuals to maintain focus and productivity while overcoming procrastination too. This is a technique that was invented in the 1990s. It was created by a man called Francesco Cirillo. Since then, this technique has quickly gained popularity as an effective technique to beat procrastination and sharpen one's powers of concentration. The theory behind this technique is that any large task (or a series of tasks) can be broken down into short, timed intervals. This technique is a time management technique that focuses on grouping tasks into twenty-five minute windows of time. For each twenty-five-minute time window, you will be allocated a five-minute break. Once you complete four twenty-five minute windows in succession, you are allowed a longer break that is usually between fifteen to thirty minutes.

This system works because instead of focusing on one particular task for an extended period of time, you actually break it down into smaller, manageable windows. It takes advantage of our brain's limited attention spans and works *with it* rather than *against* it. Also, with the smaller time frame, you will be less tempted to break away and do other unwanted tasks such as checking your email, going through social media, or any other distracting activity. Through the Pomodoro Technique, you will find that you end up getting your tasks completed due to this newfound sense of urgency, you will be able to focus on the task at hand, you avoid multitasking entirely, reduce your stress levels, and you will also increase your determination and your ability to concentrate in completing a task. This technique is easy to implement too, because all you need is a timer.

Getting started with the Pomodoro Technique is easy enough:

- **Step 1: Choose A Task -** Start by choosing a task, or series of tasks, that you want to accomplish for the day.

- **Step 2: Set Your Timer -** When you're ready to begin, set the timer for twenty-five minutes (you could also set it to forty-five minutes once you have worked your way up). Continue working on your task with no distractions until your timer goes off. Do not keep checking your timer, but instead, train yourself to concentrate on the task at hand. The timer will beep when it is time.

- **Step 3: Take Your Break -** Once the timer goes off, reward yourself by taking a short break for five minutes. It is important that you get up during this break. Don't take your break at the same spot you were working from. Get up, stretch, move around, walk around, do anything that gets you away from the desk during that period.

- **Step 4: After Four Cycles, Take A Longer Break** - Once you have completed four Pomodoro cycles, you can take a longer break for about twenty minutes.

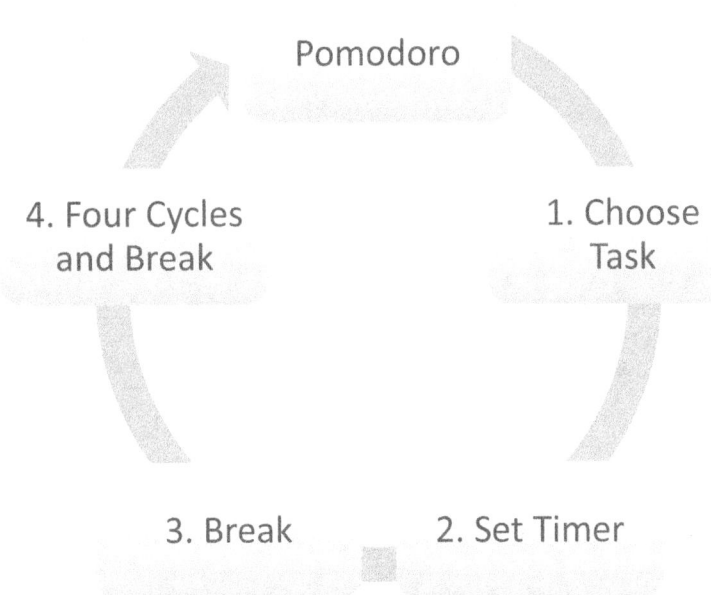

That is all there is to it. It is an excellent mechanism for training your powers of focus. The shorter time blocks will eventually build up your discipline to sit through a task without the urge to give in to the interruptions and distractions. During your Pomodoro cycles, do your best to limit and, if possible, eliminate all distractions. Put your phone on either airplane mode or do not disturb mode. The whole point of this exercise is to train your brain to master the capacity to maintain twenty-five minutes of intense focus. If you're able to, you can increase it to forty-five minutes before taking a break if you really want to challenge yourself. But twenty-five minutes is more than good enough to get you started.

Chapter 5

Getting Rid of Other Common Distraction Factors

Getting distracted is all too easy these days. We can easily get distracted when we work from home, and we can easily get distracted when we work in an office environment too.

The Science Behind Distraction

You wake up, slowly rising from your bed, already thinking about the day's tasks. As you get into work, you tell yourself, *"Okay, I'm going to finish this report today. No excuses."* You start typing and clicking between tabs when you suddenly get peppered with small interruptions. Your Facebook gets a notification, and then a few minutes later, your phone buzzes with dinner plans. A few minutes after that, your colleague swings by asking you what you'd like to go for lunch with the team. Once you settle that, you swing back to your report, but then, you get an email from your boss asking for a spreadsheet.

Before you know it, it's lunchtime, you go out, have a meal with the team, come back determined to finish the report. You look at how far you're done- you barely even completed a full page, but you've been interrupted half a dozen times! Does this sound like what you go through? These distractions result in people taking longer to complete a task. Research conducted by researchers from George Mason University says that interruptions not only take up time but they also decrease the quality of a person's work.

Previous research done on the impact of interruptions was focused more on starting, stopping, and resuming a task, and it's usually measured by time and errors made. However, research from George Mason University aims to study the effect that interruptions have on the overall quality of the tasks. George Mason University is one such science-based research done on distraction. Here are other science-backed information on how and what distraction can do to one's productivity and other areas of life:

Cyrus Foroughi, United States Naval Research Laboratory

Cyrus conducted a self-based study on distractions. He looked into the number of distractions and interruptions he experienced on a calm Monday morning. He said that within a two-hour span between 8 am to 10 am, he received one phone call, five text messages, two messages on his GChat, and six emails. Also, a fellow graduate student wandered into his room to strike up a conversation. All this on a relatively early Monday morning when the campus was still barren and quiet, and a less likely time to be interrupted.

He presented this information to researchers who were interested in how small interruptions such as this affected the quality of a person's work. In order to delve into this topic even more, researchers required a task where quality could be measured beyond the number of errors made or the time it took to complete a task. They needed to select a complex and creative task that uses common real-world scenarios, and it also required research subjects to draft and write an essay.

The Interrupted Essay Studies

Two studies were conducted among fifty college students. They were asked to write a total of three essays each based on stand college essay prompts by the College Board. They were each given twelve minutes to plan and outline their essays on paper, and then another twelve minutes to write using a computer. During this time, students were randomly interrupted at different intervals with unrelated puzzle tasks such as unscrambling words, solving math problems, and other issues.

The participants were told to complete as much of the interruption tasks as possible during the 60-second interruptions before they switched back to their essays. The interruptions took place for two of the three essays so that each student managed to complete at least one essay in one of these three conditions:

- No interruptions
- Interruptions during the planning phase
- Interruptions during the writing phase

Once the exercise was completed, they were assessed by two trained graders using a scale of zero to six taken from the College Board Essay Scoring Guide. These essays were analyzed for the total number of words written, as well as the accuracy of the interruption tasks. In the second experiment conducted, participants were given twenty minutes instead of twelve to complete their essays. During this time, participants were randomly interrupted in between writing these essays. The results? No participants scored higher when interrupted compared to the controlled group. Almost every student who was interrupted scored badly, a total of ninety-six percent had bad grades compared to 4 percent that stated the same.

This analysis also showed that when participants had to manage interruptions with the current tasks at hand, they ended up writing fewer words. A drastic change in the number of words was seen when participants wrote fewer words when interruptions took place in the writing phase, not just the planning or outline phase.

Researchers say that this could have happened because the brain just takes time to refocus, and this means people also take time to align their thoughts and attention back to the tasks that they were doing. Researchers also show that there's evidence that working memory processes also have a vital role in ensuring how we bounce back from interruptions.

Christopher Draheim's Cognitive Skills Research
Another study took place to assess the brain's capacity for multitasking. This time, a team of scientists from the Georgia Institute of Technology led by Christopher Draheim showed how the difference in a person's cognitive skills impacted their job performance, productivity, and safety in important ways.

Draheim says that everyone wants to do their personal best in their jobs because failing to do so will have major economic and mental consequences. He says that understanding that we all have limited attentional resources in working memory will help with pursuing our personal best and enable employees to seek out candidates to minimize the potential losses. It also helps applied psychologists to create better practices and assist employers in creating job situations where switching tasks is facilized while minimizing mistakes.

How Distraction Has Become A Problem

As science has shown, distraction can lead to several problems, be it productivity, quality of work as well as lifestyle. People who struggle with distraction also have issues dealing with relationships, work, education, and just general every component of their lives.

However, these struggles are more manageable with awareness and treatment strategies. It is always important to equip yourself with the right information that can help you create a plan to prevent or lessen any financial, emotional, and negative repercussions that could arise, like losing a job.

So how can distraction affect your life? Here are some negative impact of distractions in our daily lives:

Loss of household income
- The distraction causes lower productivity, affecting the quality of our work and resulting in unfavorable results.
- People who are easily distracted also end up stressed as they struggle with having to meet different deadlines and not utilizing the time they had to finish their tasks
- This stress also leads to an internal struggle with shame and guilt, including having to work much harder to meet the problems of their productivity
- Stress-induced illness – A study on the occurrence of distraction concluded that at least 24% of employees

- on sick leave as a result of stress-related illness met the criteria for Attention Deficit Disorder
- Stigma – The social rejection of friends, name-calling, missed promotions, harassment, and dismissal of employment are just a few examples when there is a chronic distraction
- absenteeism, high rate of error, inability to change, and lack of performance.
- Due to the negative out of how distractions impact our performance at work, this could lead to disciplinary actions taken by employers such as reprimands, suspensions, demotions, loss of pay, and dismissal.
- Being distracted leads to the loss of productivity, and this will then affect a person's self-confidence. It can erode as time goes by, what with the continuous loss of jobs, consistent trouble at work- all these cause traumatic experiences for the individual.

Mood changes
- An adult could also experience temporary mood instability when they get distracted easily. The brain and mind would need to switch back and forth from intense focus to interruption, and the inability to complete tasks on time could make people frustrated and annoyed by their own lack of willpower.
- People who are easily distracted tend to have chronic mood problems.

Motivation to continue
- People who are easily distracted are only motivated when there is something that interests them.
- However, feeding into this energy for too long may end up making it hard for them to find things that are interesting or exciting.

Hard to sleep

- Trouble falling asleep is also a symptom connected with someone who is distracted because of their active mind.
- A mind that keeps wandering to different things decreases the brain's ability to slow down and rest, as it is always tinkering with different thoughts and ideas and getting easily distracted.
- Or they could often feel tired but are unable to sleep because of insomnia and negative thoughts.
- They wake up through the night or may even sleep too long.

Teamwork
- Distraction also leads to a higher tendency to procrastinate.
- People who are easily distracted also have issues with disorganization, planning, and managing work.
- They find it hard to focus on a task at hand at a given time, often leading to a poor estimation of the time needed to accomplish some tasks and this results in submitting their work at the last minute.
- This poor estimation, lack of ability to concentrate, and poor on-time delivery leads to bigger issues with the team they work with.
- In situations where members must work fast to complete tasks and meet deadlines for projects and assignments.
- The inability to transfer knowledge, learning new skills and failure to follow through can cause commitment issues that are detrimental to the workplace.
- Team members who complete their tasks on time end up having to help or finish the tasks of their co-workers who have trouble focusing or those who have issues with time management.

Productivity
- People who get distracted easily could struggle to stay focused, and can get easily distracted, especially in

today's workplace, where you'd have to juggle so many tasks at once.
- As research has shown, these distractions will lead to an increase in making mistakes.
- Challenges affecting their prioritizing, organizing as well as planning will have an impact on their productivity.

Burnout
- Burnouts as a result of distraction not only require rest, but it also requires a restructuring of their organizational skill sets such as project management and time management.
- People who suffer from burnout as a result of distraction need to focus on improving their work processes, managing their distractions at work as well as identifying how they change their way of working to reduce these distractions.

Family
- Distraction also results in a member of the family requiring more time, more preparation, and more resources.
- It is not uncommon that more tension in marital and family life is often associated with these elevated demands.
- Distraction resulting in job loss also increases the challenges linked to the financial burden.
- A distracted partner often showcases little attention towards loved ones, seeming distant and not enjoying the company of being around friends and family.
- They often seem to be lost in the moment.

Distractions come in many forms, from big and obvious distractions to little interruptions that we don't seem to notice. These are some of the distractions that can pull us away from what is important:

- Ambient noise
- Buzz and chimes from our electronic devices
- Active conversations with colleagues
- The household organization, lack of space
- Information overload from displays materials
- Cell phone use (talking, texting, gaming, social media use)
- Mind-wandering, rumination
- Physiological discomfort due to temperature, body positioning
- Fatigue due to overtime or shift work
- Lack of maintenance on machines, equipment, and even work processes
- Weather and climate
- Looking for irrelevant objects in the environment (birds, animals)
- Automobiles sounds and pedestrians
- Inability to focus due to personal stress factors
- Cluttered environment
- Mind focused on other unrelated and unfinished tasks (not completing tax submissions in time)
- Pets and animals in the background
- Not eating well, not eating enough, or eating too much
- Surrounding yourself in a noise environment, with people who are easily distracted

The Underestimated Distraction You Didn't Think Of

Do you know what the biggest and the most overlooked distraction factor that most people don't think about? *Laziness*. Yes, laziness is the ultimate distraction factor that often gets overlooked. Think about how good it feels lounging about, doing nothing, scrolling through your social media feed or binge-watching your favorite series on Netflix. A little *too good,* perhaps. We have all had those days where we felt like doing nothing. Everyone experiences a couple of lazy days every now and again, and that's perfectly normal. We work hard, we undergo stressful times and daily situations, long hours of work can take a heavy toll on us both physically and mentally, and every now and again, we need a couple of lazy days or more to recharge the batteries and indulge in some quality time by ourselves. But why do some people struggle with laziness more than others?

We live in a society that praises work and never-ending activity. This is why we have been led to believe that we need to be busy all the time in order to feel useful, and it is also the reason why we feel guilty when we take some time off to indulge in ourselves. It is a shame that rest and recovery have become things that we are made to feel guilty for, especially since rest and recovery are important components to developing better focus levels. Laziness is when a person is unwilling to expend any energy doing anything, specifically when they have been given a task at hand to do. When the task is especially thought to be either difficult, consume too much effort, or if it just makes the person who has been tasked with it uncomfortable, they find themselves unwilling to put any effort or energy into getting the job done. The thing is, there is a difference between laziness and feeling tired from having too much going on.

Laziness has gone by many names over time. Some would call it idleness, some call it slothfulness, indolence, lethargy, and many more. No matter what name you call it, one thing is for sure, it all boils down to one similar characteristic. Laziness will make you unwilling to expend any extra energy and put in the work to do something, even though you may be perfectly capable of doing so. You just simply choose not to do it. Laziness can quickly become a behavioral pattern if you indulge in it far too often, and the thing about laziness is, it quietly creeps in and takes control of you, and you won't even realize it until it's too late and it becomes hard to break out of that pattern of behavior. It is a vice that takes over without you even being aware of it, and that is what makes it dangerous. Chronic laziness is when this type of behavior has become a long-term pattern, and the individual's productivity is severely affected because of it. Chronic laziness is a difficult pattern to break out of, once it has a hold of you, and you're going to have to work twice as hard to overcome it, and that can be difficult to do, seeing as how everything around us today is designed to make our lives as easy as possible.

After a long and tiring day, our bodies naturally just feel like shutting down and we have no motivation to do anything else except to just take a break and relax because we feel burned out. In that state of exhaustion, we're too tired to even think, let alone do anything else, even if there may be an important task at hand which needs to be sorted out. It is easy to fall into a lazy pattern of behavior, especially after a long day at work, because your body and mind are worn out from the day, but it is important to keep active and make yourself do at least one activity or two so you don't start to fall into this pattern of behavior. Procrastination is a direct pathway to laziness because it encourages you to indulge in that lazy feeling. It is a state of mind that is hard to break out of, and the more you postpone the things that need to be done, the less likely you're going to feel like you want to do them. Not everyone likes to live a life that is organized and detailed down to the minute. Some people just like to go with the flow and see where the day leads them too. This unplanned lifestyle can be a cause of laziness that they could end up spending aimless hours on social media, binge-watching movies and TV shows online, or even just lounging on the sofa texting for hours. Spending countless hours being inactive in one spot like that is being lazy, and the worst thing is you don't even realize how much time has passed when you're indulging in those activities. Before you know it, a whole day could go by where all you have done is get off the sofa to fix yourself something to eat and nothing more. No wonder we find it so difficult to concentrate these days.

If laziness is distracting you from being able to concentrate on what you need to do, then there is only one thing to do. You need to overcome this distraction factor, of course. Having an off day every now and then to recharge your batteries is fine, but laziness is not exactly the best thing for you when it happens too often. It's time to kick the habit in the butt once and for all so you can reclaim your time and learn to stop procrastinating. It's time to break the habit, get productive again, concentrate better, and get things done. To do that, this is what you need to do:

- **Don't Be Intimidated by Your Tasks -** Remember how most people experience a fear of failure? Well, this is not necessarily limited to big goals alone. Smaller, everyday tasks can also feel intimidating when they appear too big to handle. For example, like making a long to-do list of twenty-items, for example. Intimidation leads to procrastination, and this is why one of the many common themes you will come across as you attempt to improve your ability to concentrate will always advise you to break your tasks down into smaller, manageable goals. A massive task looks more off-putting than a smaller one, doesn't it? The minute you start to feel overwhelmed is the minute you lose any motivation, and then you feel like procrastinating and eventually feel too lazy to get it done. What do you do if you're tasked with a job that feels like far too much work? Just like the Pomodoro technique, break it down into smaller assignment goals. Instead of looking at it like one big task, break it down into smaller segments, and set a goal for yourself each day how much you want to accomplish.

- **Create Your Own Energy** - Avoiding work because you feel too tired? Find it hard to concentrate because you don't have enough energy to be productive? These are common distraction factors when you're battling with laziness. Energy and motivation are never going to fall into your lap, therefore, you have to find ways to create your own energy. Find energy by finding inspiration to keep going.

- **Open the Door to Opportunities** - Do you save your hardest tasks until the very end because, well, you dread doing it? It turns out this bad habit could be getting you in trouble. Putting off your hardest tasks is going to box you into a corner. Flip your schedule around and work on the hard tasks first. The hardest assignments are the ones we always feel like procrastinating on the most. As tempting as it may be to forget about them until you absolutely need to, they have to be tackled eventually. If you've found yourself prone to procrastinating the harder assignments in the past and leaving them to the very last minute, try switching things around and start with the hard stuff first. At the start of the day is when we have the most energy and fuel, so start your day with the hardest jobs first. If you have several hard tasks to do, pick on to work on for that day, and commit to getting it done. When you're done with that hard task, move on to smaller, more doable tasks until the end of your work day. The next morning, repeat the process by selecting another hard task and starting your day off with that again. When you get the hard stuff out of the way, you find you feel much happier, lighter and things seem more manageable somehow for the rest of the day, and it becomes much easier to concentrate and stay focused on smashing through the rest of your to-do list.

- **Identify Your Pressure Points** - When you feel a tremendous amount of stress or pressure, it can make it difficult to concentrate. If you are feeling the pressure or stress from the seemingly endless workload you have, identify the main cause of your stress first, and then do something to fix it. Overcome your pressure *before* you start work. One good approach is to try a little quiet time and meditation if you are feeling stressed before a task. Spend ten to fifteen minutes in quiet solitude to calm the mind. A calm and clear mind will have a much better time concentrating than a mind that feels like it is about to explode from pressure at any time.

- **Switch Gears** - Your brain is re-awaked whenever you switch gears. On the days where you feel you might need a little extra help concentrating, try switching things up and rotating between the tasks or routine you would normally go through.

More Tried and True Techniques to Boost Your Ability to Concentrate

Want even more techniques to boost your ability to concentrate? Then follow the recommendations on this list below:

- **Start Earlier Than Usual** - If you haven't already developed the habit of starting work at a certain time during the day, now is a good time to start. Once you have built this habit of starting work at a certain time (this should be easier to accomplish when you're working in an office), aim to start at least fifteen minutes *earlier* than you normally would. That extra bit of time in the morning is going to make a big difference in your workflow. You could dedicate those extra fifteen minutes to getting organized and getting a head start on your tasks. That way, you'll be well ahead of schedule, and this is going to give you a little triumphant burst of energy.

- **Give Memory Games a Try** - Having to memorize stuff also forces you to concentrate on what you're doing to be successful at committing it to memory. These games call for intense focus if you want to win the game. This is a fun way to get in some mental training because these interactive games can easily be played anywhere on the go, and they're usually fun and interactive. Memory games are an excellent way to help you exercise your mental muscles and train your brain to enhance its powers of focus over time. If memory games are not your thing, there are other memory techniques that you could employ. If you prefer to read, train yourself to memorize at least one inspirational passage, quote, or saying each week as part of your memory strengthening exercises. Another thing you could do is perhaps try a passage out of your favorite book, and maybe a poem or two.

- **Never Neglect the To-Do List** - Making a to-do list may seem like an extra hassle, but you would be surprised at just how effective it can be for keeping you on track. Preparing a to-do list is how you become the master of your time instead of letting time master you. From the moment you wake up in the morning, that is when your day begins, and it is from this point onwards that you need to begin effectively planning and managing your time well. Effective time management is going to involve several different aspects of your day, among which could include setting goals, planning tasks, and preparing a to-do list to keep you organized, delegating responsibilities, setting your priorities, and determining how much time to allocate to the tasks you have based on importance. If your routine prior to this was to just wake up in the morning and go with the flow or a general idea of what needs to be done that you made a mental note of, this is about to change. All it requires is a small tweak in your routine to bring about big changes in your ability to concentrate and productivity as a bonus.

- **Be Patient, Adaptable, and Flexible -** It is a shame that some people give up before they have had a chance to accomplish their goals. The reason they give up is because they are too impatient for change to happen. Impatience is your brain's worst enemy and a distraction factor. When you start focusing on how things are not moving as fast as you would like them too, that's all you're going to be able to think about. Being impatient is going to lead to the desire to want to quit. The more you obsess about it, the more precious time you lose. Time that you could have spent doing something productive, leading you one step closer to your goal. Any goal that is worth achieving is not going to happen quickly, most of the time. It is also important that you be open and willing to change when the moment comes. Sometimes, life will throw a curveball at you and put you at risk of getting distracted. To stay focused and concentrate on the goal at hand, you need to be willing to adapt and be flexible. Be willing to change when it is necessary, and this willingness to change will make your brain less resistant. When there is less resistance at work, staying focused becomes a lot easier to do. Whenever you're tempted to quit, remind yourself that it is not an option. If the option to give up is always somewhere in your mind, the temptation will always be there. Once you start something, make it a commitment to yourself that you're not going to stop until you see it all the way to the end.

- **Manage Your Time Better** - Managing your time better is not as difficult to begin as you may think. The foundation begins by first sitting down and taking a long, hard look at how you are currently spending your time. Evaluate it with honesty, because only then will you be able to see where improvement needs to be made. Evaluate how you spend the time that you have right now. Effective time management encompasses several different aspects, among which include setting deadlines, setting your goals and objectives to be achieved per task, effectively planning for each task, being able to delegate responsibilities when needed, determining which tasks should be prioritized above all other tasks. Each task should be accompanied by a goal that you want to achieve by the end of this task. This gives you something to concentrate on. Setting goals is important. Goal setting helps you give you a direction to head towards. Just like driving. When you get into a car, do you drive around aimlessly, unsure of where to go? That's what goal setting is. When you know where you're going, it makes it easier to get there quicker and more effectively with a better ability to concentrate and focus.

- **Learn to Recognize Your Work Cycles** - Another secret to better ability to concentrate is to understand the way that you work. Do you perform your best work in the morning or in the evening? Are you someone who feels sluggish and slow in the afternoons compared to the mornings? When you understand what makes you tick, that is going to help you plan out your day more productively, and in doing so, you are maximizing your powers of focus during the hours when you are at your peak performance.

- **Think of Noise-Cancelling Gear As Lifesavers** - Noise-cancelling headphones are probably the best invention when it comes to trying to stay focused and concentrate. These are going to be your best friend when it comes to blocking out external distractions. Especially when you frequently find yourself working in a noisy environment. Invest in a good pair of noise-canceling headphones that do a good job of blocking out at least ninety-percent of the noise. If calm, relaxing, soothing music helps you focus better, you get to listen to those tunes through your headphones instead of the chatter and the buzz that's going on around you. If you're going to have to listen to noise anyway, it might as well be a noise that helps you concentrate and not distract you.

- **Switch to Full-Screen Mode** - Another bad habit that we have developed thanks to this multitasking generation is working with multiple tabs open on the computer at the same time. Multiple tabs is still a form of multitasking, and it is a distraction. To narrow your field of focus, try working in full-screen mode on every task that you do on your computer. This kills two birds with one stone. It stops you from getting distracted by anything else on your computer, and it encourages you not to multitask too. When you go full screen, you're forced to only look and focus on whatever it is that is in front of you. Any files and folders on your desktop are kept out of view, and so are any extra tabs or browsers you may have open.

- **Don't Work On An Empty Stomach** - Paying attention is hard when you're distracted by the hunger pangs that go on in your stomach. Finding that balance where you're not too full or too hungry is the challenge, but it is important to find a balance that works for you or this is always going to be a problem. Hunger is not necessarily attributed to a lack of food either. Being thirsty gives the same signals that often get mistaken for hunger. But this can be a challenging problem to balance since you don't want to be too full either, given that an over-fed brain lulls your ability to focus.

Chapter 6

Creating A Working System Just for You

If only we had more hours in a day. How many times have we had that thought? While it is true that time management and efficiency have a part to play in our ability to get more things done in a day, it is pretty obvious by now that sustaining your focus for prolonged periods is ultimately the only way to succeed in any goal that you go on to set for yourself. You've come so far already by reading all the chapters this book has to offer, and now you have come to the final stage. This is the stage where you learn how to hone in on your focus, make it laser-sharp, and finally take back the control that smartphones and technology have stripped away from you. We are all limited by the same twenty-four hours in a day. If we want to get one step ahead in life, the only way is to learn how to master the power of focus. Without this fundamental core trait, all the tips, strategies, and techniques you have learned thus far are not going to do you any good. As effective as every tip in this book has been, it is not going to matter if you don't learn how to master your ability to concentrate. To do this, you need to create a working system just for you. A functional, working system that suits you is the only way to cure yourself and make every tip you have learned up to this point about curing your inability to focus count for something.

Staying on track to complete tasks is not a walk in the park for a lot of people. It can prove to be quite challenging when you are surrounded by distraction. In today's world, there are more distractions coming from a single smartphone more than anything else. Every ding, buzz, and ring, we immediately turn to our phones and go down the rabbit hole of social media posts, tweets, blog articles, and videos. The ability to focus is the defining difference between success and failure. The art of having the ability to concentrate and focus is similar to your mental muscle and physical muscle. You need to keep building it and working on it. The more you do it, the stronger it gets.

Optimizing Your Mind and Body for Better Your Ability to Concentrate and Focus

The good news for all of us is that we can always improve our mental focus, but it's not an easy or quick task. It takes some real and consistent effort, and this includes making necessary changes in our daily habits. Battling the fragmentation of attention is a battle that many people long to overcome. You've already taken the first step in admitting that there was a problem, and more importantly, you're willing to do something to fix the problem. Want to optimize your mind and body towards better focus and the ability to concentrate? Then you, my friend, need to follow these steps:

- **Start by Assessing Your Mental Focus** - Before we begin, it's always best practice to know where we are in terms of your ability to concentrate and focus. Your focus is good if you find it easy to stay alert and set clear goals. Your focus is good if you know it's better to break up tasks into smaller parts, and you take short breaks, and then get back to work. Your focus needs improvement if you get distracted easily, you find it hard to tune out distractions, you daydream regularly, and you find it hard to track your progress. Which statements above best represent you? If you think you correspond more to needing improvements, then you need to work on increasing your ability to concentrate. However, if you find your ability to concentrate good, it doesn't hurt to practice a little bit more to make it even better.

- **Cut Out the Distractions** - This is definitely an obvious solution. You need to limit your distractions, but the thing is, people underestimate just how many distractions they usually have in a single moment. These intrusions can be anything from your pet dog barking all day to co-workers dropping by to chat. What can you do then? Well, for one thing, the night before, list the tasks you need to do the next day, from the hardest to the easiest. Detail where you would be doing this and what time you think would be an ideal time to complete all of these tasks. List out the distractions you feel may take place. Listing this information out will help you visualize your opportunities and enable you to set a specific time and place within this window to be left alone to do what you need to do. Find a place that reduces these distractions to help you concentrate even more.

- **Apply the Pareto Principle** - This is also known as the 80/20 rule. The Pareto Principle was created by a man named Pareto, who went and studied various types of systems, and he discovered that eighty percent of the results are always produced by twenty of the system. Within organizations, it turns out that eighty percent of the results are being produced by twenty percent of the people. The same principle can be applied to your distraction factors. You want to shine the spotlight on the factors that are the most detrimental to your ability to focus and the factors that are the most distracting in your life. What you want to find out are the twenty percent elements that are detrimental to eighty percent of your ability to focus. There is a very good chance that your smartphone is one of your biggest culprits, with constant notifications and updates from social media and your emails. Checking your phone for those small dopamine doses is too alluring and tempting. Netflix, rambunctious roommates, noisy neighbors, distracting colleagues at the office, there could be a whole list of distraction factors, depending on when and where you are trying to concentrate. This is why it is important to develop a working system in place that will minimize your temptations and the energy that you use to resist them. Take your trusty pen and paper and spend the next five minutes after you read this writing down anything that you would consider a distraction. You should be able to come up with a list of at least twenty items. Next, you want to rate each of your distraction factors. Rate them on a scale of one to ten, depending on how powerful you think that distraction is. You will then systematically work through your list. First, you want to narrow down your top five most distracting factors from that list of twenty. If your smartphone and social media are in your top five, what you can do to minimize the temptation, and the energy you expend trying to resist this temptation, would be to turn off all notifications. Disable all your notifications when you need to work, except for phone calls and text messages.

- **Shine the Spotlight on Your Resources** - You might think that multitasking will enable you to get more things done, but not everyone is good at multitasking. Also, some tasks require full attention and focus. Again, look at your list of things and decide which need to be done with the utmost attention and how long you'd need to do it. Your goal here is to improve your mental focus to make the most of your resources. So instead of spreading your mental focus, focus it like a spotlight, shining on one specific task at a time, and shine it on your hardest task first. Give your full attention to one task before moving to the next.

- **Live In The Moment -** You've probably heard the term 'being present. To be present means putting away any distractions either in physical, emotional, or mental form and just engaging your mind, body, and soul towards the current moment. Every time you feel your mind wandering to what could have been, snapback from it and tell yourself that you cannot change the past, but you can decide how your future (even if it is the next few minutes) would be if you concentrated long enough to complete your tasks.

- **Practice Mindfulness -** Mindfulness is definitely a topic that takes center stage in practically all kinds of productivity methods and systems out there, and for good reason, too. Mindfulness meditation has been found to improve focus and attention. Even meditating for 5 minutes every day has shown to improve focus for 20 minutes, helping people stay productive and consistent in their tasks. Mindfulness enables people to stay focused on a task longer and become more efficient. It all starts with learning how to meditate and practicing easy, deep-breathing exercises.

- **Optimize Your Environment -** The optimal work environment is going to differ from one person to the next. This is because we all have a different style of working. While it is fine to draw inspiration from others, you should ideally avoid trying to copy anyone's style one hundred percent. What works for them might not be what works in a similar way for you. You want to experience the full benefit of your working system, and this is why it needs to be customized according to your personal style. Some people, for example, like working to the background noise of a busy coffee shop. They have no trouble maintaining their focus this way. Someone else might prefer to work in a quiet library, while others prefer to work in the comfort of their own home and their pajamas. Introverts tend to prefer silence and solitude, while extroverts fancy the opposite. There is no hard and fast rule about what makes a perfect work environment. You will need to experiment a little here and there to find something that works best for you. Whether you prefer quiet solitude or a little bit of background noise, there are certain fundamentals that an optimized work environment should have. The first should be minimal distractions. This means that when you are setting up your workstation, you should position yourself in such a way that your immediate periphery has limited distractions. For example, avoid sitting in front of the TV, or in an area where people are walking in and out all the time. Don't have your phone in front of you or in your pocket. Put it in your bag, in a desk drawer, or in another room. You will be amazed at how this simple trick is going to be so effective at helping your ability to concentrate. The second fundamental is that your environment should be conducive to extended periods of work. You want to be sure that you can sit in your environment for as long as you need without running into issues. Finally, the next fundamental is to set up an environment that is comfortable. Get a supportive chair, stools to rest your feet comfortably, and some people even prefer standing while they work at a standing desk. It all comes down to what your personal preference is, there is no hard and fast rule, and remember that it does not have to be perfect. You should do whatever works best for you.

- **Taking Short Breaks** - We've covered the importance of this in the Pomodoro method. Focus starts to break down if you try to stay on it for a long period of time. It becomes even more strenuous to devote your mental resources to a task for a long period of time, and this affects performances. Taking a brief break shifts the attention of the mind elsewhere, and when you get back on track, it helps the mind shift back to focus, thus improving your ability to concentrate. An occasional mental break such as drinking water, stretching, breathing deeply for five minutes, or just taking a short walk gives the brain and body a short moment of respite before going back to the tasks at hand.

- **Respect Your Work Zone** - If you are living with other people, it is important to let them know about your work zone and the importance of respecting this zone. It is critical to limit distractions, including the distractions that come from other people. If you find yourself interrupted frequently, then you are probably not in an optimal work environment. Speak to them and explain what you are trying to do and why it matters that you stay focused when you're working. Let them know you would appreciate it if they could work together with you by respecting your work zone and staying away from that area during the hours they know you need to get something done.

How to Train Your Brain for Laser-Sharp Focus

Now that we have a better idea of how to optimize focus and attention, we can look into training our brain to stay laser-sharp focused on our tasks. But before you do that, you need to reframe the way that you think about failure. There is something to be learned from every experience that you go through. This even includes a task as simple as washing the dishes. Successful individuals who have mastered the art of concentration have also developed a very special skill. They have learned how to reflect on their experiences and think about the lessons that they can draw from it. What did that experience teach them about themselves? What did it teach them about others? How would these lessons be useful to them in moving them forwards toward achieving their goal?

This is one of the many ways they trained their minds to focus with laser-sharp clarity on their goal without being distracted by all the other factors around them.
Here are some ways to do that:

- **Get Enough Sleep** - Not having enough sleep makes us tired fast. This leads to a decrease in your ability to concentrate, it leads to making more mistakes, it decreases our ability to perform. All of this happens because sleep contributes to healthy cognitive functions. Getting eight hours of uninterrupted sleep helps us think clearly and make better decisions. It also helps us eat better, making better choices of eating foods that help accelerate focus.

- **Use the ABC System** - The ABC method is a system created by Harvard researchers for productivity and focus purposes. A is for Aware, B for Breathe, and C is for choice. You begin by becoming aware of your options- to pay attention or to remain distracted. Next, breathe and relax by focusing on what you choose- focus or distraction.

- **Meditation** - Mindful meditation is essential to the mind and body. Meditating daily for even five minutes allows the brain to go into a mental retreat. One of the most calming exercises around meditation, a practice that has numerous benefits, among which include helping you regulate your emotions. Spend a few minutes in a day meditating because it is important to stop and calm the busy mind every now and again. You have a lot going on in your life, especially with recovering from stress. Meditation teaches you control over your emotions by teaching you how to deliberately slow down your thoughts through mindfulness. When you come out of this retreat, you are more focused, and your cognitive functions are accelerated. Sitting in silence and allowing yourself to filter through your thoughts is powerful. It can dramatically change the way that you think, and it can change your perspective. It also gives you the freedom to focus on what truly matters to you.

- **Build A Commitment to Change** - This method is to visualize and make a promise to yourself. Think about what outcome you want to see or feel or reap by becoming more focused and attentive. Let's start by doing a little exercise. Get a pen and paper and write down your personal mission statement:
    - What are the things that are most important to you?
    - What are the things that you want to do in this life?
    - What are your values and beliefs?
    - What are your personal goals?
    - What are your professional goals?

    When doing this exercise, remember that creating your commitment to change isn't a one-time thing that's set in stone. Give yourself that opportunity to review your mission statement annually and see if it has resulted in aligning positively with your life, career, jobs, and relationships. Make adjustments if necessary. The change will never be achieved without any commitment. We need to have a strong commitment that engages us to change and to sustain.

- **Setting Goal Reminders** - If you find it easy to get sidetracked from your goal, then having a reminder might be what you need. Surround yourself with these reminders. That way, you don't have the opportunity to forget them. Create a vision board. Write down your mission and stick it around your home or in your cubicle at work. Stick these reminders on your mirrors, next to your bed, or make them your desktop or mobile wallpaper. Every time you look at these reminders, you'll remember what it is you're working hard for and why you're committing yourself to master the ability to concentrate for prolonged periods and why it is going to make a difference in your life. Remind yourself why you are working so hard to switch on your focus.

- **Adopt the *Zanshin* Philosophy** - The *Zanshin* philosophy can be used in many different aspects of life, and it is a great mantra to remember when you are on the path towards staying focused. The *Zanshin* philosophy is the art of living with alertness, whether or not your goals have been achieved. Everything does not end the minute you win the battle. The battle really ends when you lose your level of commitment. When you get lazy and when you stop improving or paying attention. Here are some areas to use Zanshin:

    - Fitness- Your fitness goal does not end when you hit your personal record. It ends when you stop. When you stop training, when you stop concentrating, when you let go, when you skip workouts or when you just lose sight of what being fit is all about.

    - Relationship- You've probably heard this one before- to be in a long term relationship or marriage requires work. Things don't end when you tie the knot- that's actually the beginning. You need to put in as much effort as you first did when you wooed your partner. Keep dating, keep complimenting, keep surprising.

    - Entrepreneurship- Your battle ends when you get cocky, and don't be too proud of your own good. Success means reinventing yourself, learning from your mistakes, looking at what you did to see how you can improve.

- **Turning Up the Heat and Going Green -** Sometimes, we need a physical change, and according to some research, warmer places help the human mind stay focused and productive. In that same vein of thought, adding plants around where you work promotes positive vibes and effects. It increases morale and promotes productivity.

- **The Forty-Second Focus On the Color Red -** The next time you feel like you need help to refocus your mind and energy, take a break and look at the color red for forty-seconds. Whether it's on a computer screen or a wall, the color red has been shown to have a major impact on focus. A study published in *Science* magazine showed that people who looked at the color red performed way better and had better memory retention when they got back to their tasks.

- **Surround Yourself with the Right People -** Training your brain to have laser-sharp focus also includes seeing *what* 'staying focused' really means. When you see someone staying focused on a task, your mind visualizes it, and it's imprinted in you, making you want to be like that too. The wrong type of person is nothing more than another form of distraction. Toxic friendships, manipulative relationships, these are distracting factors because they pull your attention away from what matters. Karl Marx put it perfectly "'Surround yourself with people who make you happy. People who genuinely care. They are the ones worth keeping in your life. Everyone else is just passing through." The key is finding the people that are good for you. If your intention is to stay focused, then sit with colleagues whom you know are focused and productive until you've finished your task.

How to Sharpen That Attention Span

This is going to be a little bit of an uphill battle for many, especially given the fact that our attention spans are getting shorter by the year. The secret to living a focused life where your ability to concentrate is not a problem is *direction*. Your life needs direction, and the direction is guided by discipline and consistency. There are things that you can do to stay true to this direction, and one of those things is to sharpen your attention span. Our attention span has a lot to do with our environment. A study by the Technical University of Denmark proved that we are being faced with more information than we were several years ago, and while we have more things to focus on, our ability to focus is diminishing. According to the study, the reason behind this shorter attention span is the urge for constant "newness" that has emerged because of the increasing volume of content. When we keep looking for what the next "new" thing is, we switch topics more frequently.

Microsoft had an interesting take on the subject too. In a 2015 study, Microsoft claimed that the average person has an eight-second attention span. In this study, they claimed that this was less than the attention span of a goldfish. That number, by the looks of it, is shrinking every year with our increasing dependence on our digital connectivity. Microsoft Canada's consumer insights lead, Alyson Gausby, pointed out that no matter what environment we find ourselves in, our survival depends on our ability to remain focused. To sharpen our attention span, we need to reduce this interference, because the right environment sometimes matters more than motivation does.

Here are simple ways to help you increase your attention span, especially at times when you need it the most:

- **Put A Stop to Multitasking** - This has been mentioned several times throughout this book, and this is the reason why. Multitasking puts a stop to your efficiency and performance. No matter what the articles you read and society will try to convince you of, the truth is that multitasking will make it *impossible* to focus. Multitasking is a fallacy, and *that* is the truth. It is the lie we have all been taught to believe that we could juggle several things at once and still achieve incredible success. Oh, it may work well in the beginning, and you feel like you're pulling off an impossible feat. Your colleagues watch with admiration, and you seem like an unstoppable force that just keeps going, going, going. It won't be long before you end up burned out, stressed out, and depleted of any mental energy needed to focus on the remainder of the work that needs to get done. Instead of trying to do several things at once, focus on one task at any given time. When you give one hundred percent of your focus to a single task at a time, the quality of your work is going to double. Perhaps even triple.

- **Work in Natural Light -** A study found that people who worked in spaces or places that had loads of natural light had less eye strain, blurred visions, and headaches. It also increased their attention span and focus.

- **Listen to Music -** Classical music is the best form of music to listen to when you want to stay focused as it triggers the part of our brain that helps us increase our attention span. People's minds tend to wander when listening to music but classical music includes a feature known as 'transitional points'- there is silence, and this triggers the mind to be aware and attentive.

- **Work Like the Athletes Do -** Imagine that you were running a race. In that race, there was only one goal, one outcome. Make it to the end and finish with a medal. While you get your body warm, stretch your muscles, and line up at the starting block, that outcome becomes the only thing on your mind. As your legs pump and your heart pounds with each step you take, all you're focused on is crossing that finish line. You keep your eyes directly in front of you as you stride closer and closer. You don't look left, you don't look right. You know that as soon as you do, you're in danger of being distracted by the other runners, possibly missing a step and tripping. This is now the work style that you need to adopt. Sharpen your attention span by looking at each task as a finish line you need to cross. Don't look left, don't look right, only look straight ahead. The only thought in your mind should be the thought of crossing that finish line, nothing else.

- **Stay Hydrated -** Our bodily functions, including our ability to focus, is only as good as what you put into your body, and hydration is at the top of that list. A study conducted by the University of Barcelona found that even mild hydration at two percent decreased attention. To stay hydrated, keep a bottle with you when you need to finish a task. Drink a few sips along the way, stretch, look up from your laptop, and after a few minutes, continue working. Tea has also been found to help with maximizing attention span. Black tea specifically contains amino acids called L-Theanine that affects the areas of the brain that control attention. Studies conducted have shown that tea drinkers have a better attention span.

- **Declutter Your Mind** - You cannot hope to concentrate well if your brain is already full of thoughts that clutter your clarity. Clutter here refers to the thoughts that serve no real benefit. Your mind fills with thoughts that do nothing to improve your life, and thoughts that have no significant contribution to your life or your wellbeing. Not every detail is going to matter, and a skill you must now develop as you work on mastering the big picture mental model is to declutter your mind and free it from all the excess information. You must be willing to let go of the details that are not important if you want to see the bigger picture. Decluttering your mind is going to eliminate the unnecessary details from your workflow, thus ensuring that you're not stuck on one problem or task for too long before moving onto the next.

- **Brain Gymnastics** - Who would have thought that deep breathing and simple exercises with your fingers could boost the function of your brain and your capacity to concentrate? It turns out that it can be more effective than we think. Developed by Yoshiro Tsutsumi, a Japanese researcher, brain gymnastics focuses on improving brain health through a short finger workout. The theory behind this is when you do finger exercises, you are improving the brain's synapses connections and firing up your neurons, all of which are great for brain function. An example of this exercise is to take a deep breath and lift your fingers (palms of your hands together) until it is at eye level.

Your fingers should be touching. Take a deep breath in through your nose and then exhale through your mouth. As you exhale, lower your right hand a bit. The fingers of your left hand should be able to cover the tops of your right hand when you do this. Use the fingers of your left hand to cover the fingers of your right hand on the exhale of your breath. It should look as if you were trying to catch your hand that was sliding down. Breathe in through your nose, and repeat everything you just did, except this time you are going to lower your left hand. Repeat this exercise fifteen times. The point of this exercise is to maintain focus on your breath as you inhale and exhale while you move your fingers. A short but effective workout in warming your brain up to focus on the task ahead.

- **Write Things Down** - Whether you are in class, in a meeting, or at a conference- take a good old pen and paper with you. Or if you have an iPad or Tablet that can help you take down notes electronically, that's good too. The idea here is to write it down by hand. Writing things down helps you listen more actively and identify important concepts. If you are using a digital device to help you take notes- turn off notifications. This way, you don't get distracted and end up checking your email or social media.

- **Prioritize Working Solo** - This is the time when being alone is going to pay off, even if you are someone who doesn't like being alone in general. The time to prioritize solo time is when you need to buckle down and concentrate. If you find yourself in a situation where you do have to work in a team or group, that group should ideally be kept small. It should be limited to no more than two people. Understandably, this is not always the case. Group discussions should be limited to only the most important details related to the project. Other than those times when you need to work in a group, working solo is a much better option for your attention span since the temptation to converse with others is going to be removed from the picture.

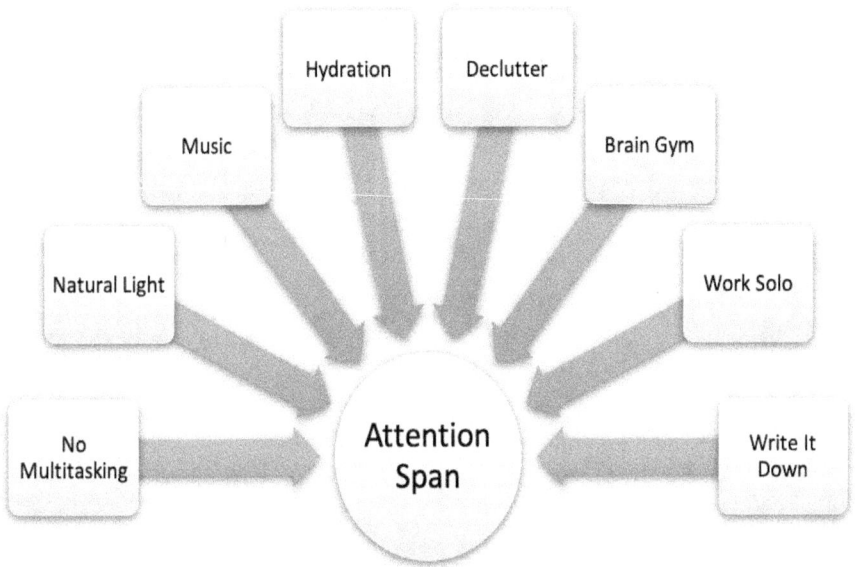

Finally, all you need to do is keep practicing all the strategies you have learned. We get better at the things we consistently continue to practice, and this includes our ability to concentrate. If you continue to keep to all advice and tips you have read in this book and apply the Pomodoro technique, you should see a noticeable improvement in your ability to concentrate in no time. As your ability to concentrate muscle grows, you can experiment with extending the cycles and try to see how long you can maintain your focus. Think of it as a personal challenge.

Getting into the groove of concentrating for prolonged periods is going to become a lot easier. By having a routine that you repeat, you are training your subconscious mind to quickly get into work mode. It is also important that you don't feel guilty about taking the breaks that you need. Yes, it is important to get work done, but it is equally important that you take the time to recuperate when you need it. Your ability to concentrate is not limitless, and avoiding burnout comes with listening to your mind and your body. Breaks are necessary, and the way that you utilize your breaks matters too. Don't forget that you are the sum of your habits, therefore, what you prioritize is going to reflect in your ability to concentrate.

Conclusion

Thank you for making it through to the end of *Boost Your Focus*, let's hope it was informative and able to provide you with all of the tools you need to achieve your goals whatever they may be.

The ability to focus and concentrate is to pick one goal, and then finish that goal before you move on to the next. Bill Gates once said that if you want to be a great software company, then you only need to be a software company, and you cannot be anything else at the same time. Multitasking is a myth, and it is time to stop believing in the false sense of productivity that it feeds you with. Dabbling in several things at once is the one habit you need to start breaking away from. All the techniques you have learned in this book are meant to help you concentrate anywhere from a few minutes to several hours if you need to. With practice, you will eventually learn how to block out all the distractions around you and concentrate anytime you need, no matter where you are.

www.ingramcontent.com/pod-product-compliance
Lightning Source LLC
Chambersburg PA
CBHW070418220526
45466CB00004B/1449